"I thank God for Mike Adams. His book is way more than an entertaining read, though it is that! It's a call to a self-righteous generation to give up imaginary causes that inflate the ego but do nothing to promote real justice in the culture. The chapters on abortion alone are worth the purchase price! If you are a conservative student or parent, read this to engage a center-left nation that would rather feel than think!"

—**SCOTT KLUSENDORF**, president
of the Life Training Institute

"Four decades ago I could have used a professor like Mike Adams who cared enough to challenge the Marxist thinking into which I fell. If you love a student who is also succumbing, this book is an ideal present. Two hours with it can awaken a propagandized brain that will otherwise wallow in two or more years of misery."

—**MARVIN OLASKY**, editor in chief of World News Group
and author of *The Tragedy of American Compassion*

LETTERS TO A YOUNG PROGRESSIVE

LETTERS TO A YOUNG PROGRESSIVE

HOW TO AVOID WASTING YOUR LIFE PROTESTING THINGS YOU DON'T UNDERSTAND

MIKE S. ADAMS

Since 1947
REGNERY
PUBLISHING, INC.
An Eagle Publishing Company • Washington, DC

Cataloging-in-Publication data on file with the Library of Congress
ISBN 978-1-62157-031-8

Published in the United States by
Regnery Publishing, Inc.
One Massachusetts Avenue NW
Washington, DC 20001
www.Regnery.com

Manufactured in the United States of America
10 9 8 7 6 5 4 3 2 1
Books are available in quantity for promotional or premium use. Write to Director of Special Sales, Regnery Publishing, Inc., One Massachusetts Avenue NW, Washington, DC 20001, for information on discounts and terms or call (202) 216-0600.

Distributed to the trade by
Perseus Distribution
250 West 57th Street
New York, NY 10107

Author's note: A small portion of what follows is adapted from material that originally appeared in my weekly column at Townhall.com but that bears repeating.

To Marilyn Adams,
a praying mother who never gave up on me

Contents

Preface

The story you are about to read is true, though the hero of our tale is a composite character, representing countless students I've taught over the years. They enroll in universities for a valuable education and instead become increasingly enraged at the world and disgusted with other people. This is unfortunate, because they are getting angry over things that aren't even true. They are misled by a miserable generation of professors acting on the principle that misery loves company.

In North Carolina, where I teach, parents who didn't get to go to college themselves work and save and sacrifice so that they can proudly send their kids to join the alleged best and brightest and be successful. But after a short time on a university campus, the kids start rejecting their parents' values—the very values that have provided for their education. Ironic, isn't it? Sometimes the parents begin to wonder whether they're making a wise investment by sending their kids to college—or at least to a secular college. Tensions arise between kid and parent, and the parent notices that the kid has stopped respecting the parent's point of view. I notice, too. When I comment on students' angry outbursts of disdain for other people, suggesting they might show a little more humility, I inevitably hear back, "You sound just like my dad."

When I began writing these letters, I didn't realize I was writing a book. In fact, when I first wrote the first letter, I was already at work on a completely different book. But after a series of encounters with students whose worldview had been soured by progressive education, I thought of all the other bright kids across the country, tens of thousands of them, who are intellectually impressionable because they *are* bright, and how they are being led astray by professors who take pleasure in making students angry and alienated. I wanted to do something to counter that.

If this account sounds personal, that's because it is. I was once one of those bright kids, lost for seventeen angry years because of professors who lured me into their reasonless angst. It almost killed me. But I survived.

Unlike most true stories, this one has a happy, if surprising, ending. Start reading and keep on reading. Don't cheat by flipping forward to the last chapter. The destination requires a journey.

PART ONE

SIGNPOSTS ALONG THE WAY

*"Rhetoric is no substitue
for reality."*
—Thomas Sowell

No, Zachary, Glenn Beck Isn't Charles Manson

Dear Zach,

I hope your semester is going well. I've been pleased to have you in my class on famous American trials (CRM 425 or "Trials of the Century"), and I'm taking the time to write in response to a remark you made during our recent discussion of the Manson case.

As you undoubtedly recall, we were discussing Charles Manson, who directed members of his "Family" to commit a series of grisly murders in 1969, and when I noted that Manson had exploited his followers through fear, you interrupted, "Sort of like Glenn Beck?"

I probably have too many pet peeves for a man of my age, and students' blurting out questions or comments without raising a hand—particularly when I am in the middle of a sentence and the comment leads the discussion astray—is one of them.

But I haven't written to scold you. I can't do that because I don't have the moral authority to do so. You see, I used to be like you. Let me explain.

A fundamentalist Baptist mother and an atheist father raised me, and when I went off to college in 1983, I declared myself an agnostic. Had I remained an agnostic, things might not have been so bad. But instead, while I was a graduate student, I declared myself an atheist. There was nothing intellectual about my decision to become an atheist; it was behavior-driven.

In 1989, I began a short career as a professional musician to help pay for school, and started experimenting with amphetamines and methamphetamines. The drugs nearly killed me. In late 1990, I had a fight with my girlfriend and suddenly found myself taking a trip to the emergency room after my heart stopped beating. That was a direct result of the pills. I later realized I also had a serious problem with alcohol.

I was passionate about being an atheist. I once told a fellow graduate student, the wife of a pastor, to "Go [rhymes with "truck"] yourself" when she tried to "witness" to me.

I adopted leftist politics to go with my atheism. The connection to the progressive worldview was clear and simple. In rejecting Christianity, I had rejected the Judeo-Christian view of man as a fallen being. Instead, I believed that we could create a utopia through politics. I felt contempt for conservative Christians who stood in the way of progress, who did not realize that man was fundamentally good and perfectible. We didn't need God; we only needed the right laws, the right people in office, and the right social conditions, and then everything would be perfect—all the world's problems would be solved.

I pretended to be an intellectual atheist, but really I had adopted this worldview because it allowed me to live a life unencumbered by morality, to sleep with a different woman every night, and not to feel bad about it—or so I thought. What really happened was that treading the path of militant liberal atheism made me an angrier and angrier person— the sort of person, in fact, who would compare a talk show host to a serial killer.

That is why I am writing to you today. I know that you have been spending a lot of time on left-wing websites like the Daily Kos and Media Matters, the latter of which is run by billionaire communist George Soros. I have also noticed that you have been increasingly virulent in your attacks on Republican politicians such as George W. Bush and Sarah Palin. Your demeanor is increasingly hostile and arrogant. It reminds me of a time in my own life when I thought I was being clever and cynical and wise.

In a nutshell, you are acting a lot like I acted when I carried the banner of progressivism, and that is why I say I lack the moral authority to look down on you. But I hope I can warn you.

Zach, you are so bright and have so much potential that I think it's a shame you are so angry at such a young age. I also think it's a shame because I know that so much of your anger stems from misinformation. That is why I plan to (at least try to) do something about it.

After the end of this semester, I will be driving out to Colorado to teach at Summit Ministries. If you're interested, I'd be happy to write to you periodically over the summer to share some of what I learned on my journey from being a progressive atheist to becoming a conservative Christian.

Meanwhile, I'll see you in class. Before I forget, congratulations on getting the highest score on our last test. Finals will be here before you know it—good luck on your exams!

How Being for Equality Makes You Better than Other People

Greetings from Manitou Springs, Colorado, Zach.

The weather outside does not bode well for the global warming apologist. It is 37 degrees here in Colorado in the middle of the afternoon in the middle of May. The light rain is expected to turn into snow this afternoon. So it's a good time to sit down at the computer and do some writing.

Congratulations on finishing CRM 425 with flying colors. I really appreciated you stopping by my office to discuss the letter I sent you at the end of the semester. This will be the first installment in the correspondence that I promised you this summer.

I'd like to use this letter to discuss a topic I have already broached with you. The comment you made—suggesting some similarities between Glenn Beck and Charles Manson—has been weighing on my mind.

I want you to know that your comment, which trivialized Manson's moral culpability, was actually not the worst comment I've ever heard about Charles Manson. That honor goes to a remark by a professor I once heard characterize Manson as a "poor little guy who got railroaded by the system."

Of course, Zach, you've heard the basic facts of the Manson case; and you know him to be guiltier than—for lack of a better term—sin. The suggestion that Manson is innocent is one of the most careless I've ever heard. Let me be blunt. It takes a Ph.D. to be brash enough to say something like that.

Make no mistake about it—your idea about Charles Manson and Glenn Beck was bad. But not all ideas are equally bad. There is a serious movement in the academy— ironically, a movement obsessed with equality in all areas of life, economically, culturally, and morally—that is much worse than the cheap shot you took in class. It's that ideology that the professor was expressing when he called Manson a "poor little guy." You've heard of Marxist economics, but you may not have heard about the approach to morality that tends to go along with it.

In economics, Marxism is a proven disaster. According to Marx, we should take from each person according to his ability and give to each person according to his need. I once illustrated the disastrous consequences of that economic policy in a column I wrote, entitled "My New Spread the Wealth Grading Policy."

I suggested that people who made an "A" on the first test really did not need the four grade points associated with a grade of "A," since it only takes a 2.0 average to graduate. So my column suggested that those with an "A" should give a grade point away to students making an "F" in order to facilitate a more equal grade distribution—one with just three levels: "B", "C", and "D."

My column also suggested that additional modifications could be made after the second exam. I specifically proposed taking a grade point away from those with a "B" test average and giving that point to those with a "D" average. That would mean everyone would have a grade of "C," which is worth the two grade points everyone needs to average in order to graduate.

Any undergraduate is capable of figuring out the point of my satire. If every student were guaranteed the exact same outcome, no student would put forth any kind of effort on class assignments or tests. Put simply, "My New Spread the Wealth Grading Policy" would destroy academic productivity and create a shoddy and embarrassing academic work product. Academic standards would plummet under such a system.

Socialism, of course, would do exactly the same thing to our economy. If every worker is guaranteed the exact same outcome—via the redistribution of wealth—then no worker will put forth a strong effort on the job. The average standard of living for the nation as a whole will plummet—or, rather, actually has plummeted wherever Marxist economics has been tried.

As a conservative, I take a far different approach to the subject of equality. I believe that our only obligation is to provide people with equal opportunity. We are not obliged to guarantee everyone an equal outcome. We cannot do so. Nor should we even try.

This is good news for you, Zach. You are much brighter than the average student. You are also much more motivated. You will soar to far greater heights if you are merely given the opportunity.

It sounds harsh to say that Marxism is for the lazy and untalented. But that is what I believe. Who else would consider mediocrity to be a satisfactory outcome?

Ironically, equality-loving socialists obviously think they're morally superior to capitalists. Which is odd, because isn't equality the whole point? Even odder, the people who call themselves Marxists are usually the same people who subscribe to cultural and moral relativism. In theory, they don't think there are any universal moral standards to judge other people by.

Just as they want economic equality, they want everyone to be on an equal moral plane. They want to believe that all people are morally equal—for example, that a brutal murderer such as Charles Manson is not particularly guilty. They dub anyone who fails to adopt their relativist views as "ethnocentric."

I once espoused this "all people and all cultures are equal" mentality. But my moral relativism came to an abrupt end one afternoon when I spent a few hours in an Ecuadorian prison. One day, in another letter, I'll tell you the whole story of how that visit changed my whole outlook on life. But right now I want to tell you the story of how an editor with an enlightened, progressive attitude didn't want me to tell that original story.

I wrote an article about that prison visit. But when I submitted the article to a human rights journal, it was nearly rejected by the editor. Two parts of the article offended her. The first was where I acknowledged that the work of Chuck Colson had piqued my own interest in prison conditions in Third World countries. The second was where I complained that the food in the prison had a very bad smell.

Her first issue with the article is of little interest. It would appear that the editor harbored some anti-Christian bigotry, which is not uncommon. But her second complaint is of greater interest, and more thought is required to dissect it.

When the editor told me that it wasn't nice to judge the foods of other cultures—including the rotten meat I saw being boiled in order to be fed to the prisoners at that

Ecuadoran prison—she was, of course, implicitly accusing me of ethnocentrism, which is defined as judging other cultures by the standards of one's own culture.

Notice that the accusation of ethnocentrism is self-defeating because it, too, is a form of ethnocentrism. You cannot accuse someone of ethnocentrism without forcing your own standards upon them—standards they do not share. Let me explain.

Ethnocentrism is a concept really only taught within the culture of sociology and anthropology departments at secular universities. The idea that you should not judge other cultures is itself a judgment, and the number of people who subscribe to it make up a very small percentage of the people on this planet. But they demand that we all live by their non-judgmental worldview, which flourishes only in certain departments of elite Western universities, even though that worldview really imposes harsh judgments on others outside their own culture.

Logic aside, there is also a serious practical reason to avoid falling into the trap of cultural relativism—it renders one completely incapable of addressing the problem of evil. It may seem chic to refrain from judging other cultures when it comes to something trivial like tastes in food or fashion. But what about something like genocide?

Are we really prepared to say that our culture today is not superior to that of Nazi Germany in the 1930s? Does anyone consider such a view to be chic?

And is it really morally sophisticated to pretend that you don't notice that the rotten meat being fed to prisoners in a hellhole of a prison smells badly? Or, coming closer to home, that you don't see any difference between a talk show host whose politics you don't agree with, and a man responsible for several gruesome murders?

We know from history that any society foolish enough to experiment with Marxism will find that the quest for equality results in a lower standard of living for all. Similarly, any society foolish enough to embrace cultural relativism will find that the quest for equality results in a lower overall standard of morality.

We all lose something when we try to place all individuals on an equal plane by embracing a general philosophy of moral relativism—or of moral equivalence, as progressives so often do in the political realm. When a progressive does something wrong, his fellow progressives blandly defend him by pointing out the flaws of the guys on the other side. If everyone is guilty, no one is guilty.

There was a reason why that professor said Charles Manson was a "poor little guy who got railroaded by the system." The professor is a political liberal who bought into the free-love philosophy of the 1960s. What Manson and the members of his hippie "Family" did makes crystal clear what a failure and a sham that whole free-love movement became. The youths of the 1960s eventually proved themselves to be the worst generation this nation has ever produced.

Manson is a vicious murderer who induced others to murder by preying upon their fears. It is both silly and wrong to call him innocent. It is also silly to compare him to Glenn Beck—a man who, whatever his flaws, has never murdered anyone.

Moral relativism fails logically. But it's very useful psychologically—for those who want to escape the possibility of ever feeling guilty, so that they may do as they please, whenever they please. I found moral relativism very convenient for this purpose when I was sleeping around and doing drugs.

But moral relativism and moral equivalence don't just help you feel equal to other, better people when actually you ought to feel bad about yourself. They also help you feel superior when, actually, you ought to feel quite ordinary. Why is it so completely typical for college students (and professors) who have adopted the Marxist program of economic equality—and the moral relativism that tends to go with it—to feel so smugly superior? Somehow their new political stand for equality makes them feel like they're better than other people—better than the families who are sending them to college, better than ordinary Americans, and, especially, better than Tea Party members, Rush Limbaugh fans, and people who watch Glenn Beck.

"The Trees"

Zach,

Speaking of people to whom leftists feel smugly superior, I'm going to write you today about Ayn Rand. In recent years, there has been a resurgence of interest in her books.

After escaping from the Soviet Union in the 1920s, Rand became a famous American playwright, philosopher, and novelist. She wrote many books, three of which I would urge you to read. The first, *We the Living*, based on her youth in early Soviet Russia, is a lot like Orwell's *1984*. The second, *The Fountainhead*, is a longer novel expounding her philosophy, which is known as objectivism. The third, *Atlas*

Shrugged, is her most famous work and includes the most complete explanation of her views on economics and morality.

As a Christian, I reject a good bit of what Ayn Rand has to say. Because she doesn't take the fall of man into account, I don't think she has a complete explanation for why capitalism works better than socialism or communism.

But Rand defends capitalism eloquently by pointing out a key flaw in socialism, and I am not at all uncomfortable recommending her books. (In fact, I have made the case for reading books whose messages I completely reject, including the original works of Marx and of Hitler. There is much to be learned from studying the works of those with whom you disagree—and much to be missed by ignoring them.)

It could take you several weeks to read those three books. Meanwhile, I want to draw your attention to a song that was written by a rock musician influenced by Ayn Rand. The artist's name is Neil Peart—a member of the band Rush. Neil is arguably the greatest rock and roll drummer who has ever lived. He is also one of the greatest songwriters.

When I was a teenager in the 1970s, "The Trees" was one of my favorite songs. I didn't know at the time that the song was a stinging indictment of socialism and communism inspired by Neil's reading of Ayn Rand novels. It's literally a song about trees—maples who "want more sunlight" and oaks who "ignore their pleas."

When I look back on it, I am somewhat embarrassed that it took me so long to figure out the symbolism behind the oak-versus-maple contrast. This is a classic Marxist over-simplification, which is intentional on Peart's behalf. There are only two classes of people, according to the worldview of Karl Marx—the haves and the have-nots or, as he called them, the "bourgeoisie" and the "proletariat." Here, the oaks are the "haves" or the "bourgeoisie," and the maples are the "have-nots" or the "proletariat."

The scenario in the song is interesting because it raises the issue of absolute versus relative poverty. When the maples claim that the oak trees grab up all the light, they are exaggerating—actually, the author of the song, Neil Peart, is exaggerating for effect. Oaks are big trees, to be sure. In my own yard, there is an oak that is 100 feet tall that will eventually grow to be about 125 feet tall. But maples are big trees, too. I have a sugar maple that is about 60 feet tall that will eventually grow about 80 feet.

Peart, quite ingeniously, shows that the have-nots are often better characterized as simply having *less* than others. Their problem is not really that they do not have enough to get by. The problem is that, in their view, the oaks are "too lofty." In other words, others have much more than they do. That is the key phrase because it reveals that covetousness, rather than true need, is what is motivating the maples. In reality, that is what always motivates collectivism.

The results of collectivism are also always predictable. In the song, the maples start by complaining; accelerate their complaints to demands; and, in the end, settle upon force to obtain what they want. The "oppression" of the oaks is replaced by a regime of strict equality, enforced by "hatchet, axe, and saw."

The end of the song is chilling because it reveals the truth about progressivism. To begin with, it's not really progressive. It's not about helping anyone get ahead, but instead about holding some people back. What's "progressive" about retarding some people's achievements?

Ayn Rand was not a Christian. She did not profess to believe in the Ten Commandments. Nonetheless, she understood that what is packaged as compassion is often really covetousness in disguise. We would do well to familiarize ourselves with her work in an age of "collective" historical amnesia.

Social Security and Racism

Zach,

In this letter I'm going to focus on the subject of racism, which is, and has been for quite some time, a hot-button issue in America. Having grown up in the South—I was born in Mississippi and raised in Texas—I have thought about the issue a lot over the years.

One thing I've noticed is that the progressive worldview gets a lot of its moral authority from the issue of racism. Even if Marxism and moral relativism are discredited by history and logic, progressives still look like the good guys when the subject of race comes up, since racial equality obviously *is* the right answer.

The problem is that the definition of racism has changed a great deal in recent years. Racism once referred to an ideology that was based on a belief in certain races' inferiority. This general inferiority was presumed to flow from inferior intellectual ability, often ascribed to genetic inferiority.

Genetic racism is a dangerous ideology. In the middle of the nineteenth century, it played a central role in America's bloodiest war. In the twentieth century, it fueled the Holocaust in Nazi Germany. But, fortunately, in the twenty-first century, its popularity is waning.

In recent decades, as old-fashioned racism based on genetics has become more and more discredited, new types of racism have been making their way into the national discourse on race. One of those alternative forms of racism is called "institutional racism."

Institutional racism is any form of racial disparity, whether created intentionally or not, that occurs within institutions. For example, if people of a given race are more likely to be imprisoned than those of other races, this would be considered a form of institutional racism—regardless of the reason for their incarceration, or the motives of the police officers and judges.

To anyone interested in understanding why racism seems, counterintuitively, to be increasing in recent years,

I recommend reading *When Prophecy Fails: A Social and Psychological Study of a Modern Group that Predicted the Destruction of the World*, by Leon Festinger, Henry Riecken, and Stanley Schachter.

In this book, the authors found that a group who predicted that the world would end on a certain date did not disband after their predicted doomsday date passed and the prophecy failed to come true—as one would intuitively expect. Instead, they continued to set numerous new dates for the world to end, even as the world kept right on going each time.

Festinger and his colleagues explained these results in terms of "effort justification," a concept flowing from cognitive dissonance theory. The idea is simple—people who had invested a lot of effort in a cause could not handle the idea that their efforts were in vain. So instead of disbanding the group, they simply set another date for the end of the world—and then another, and another.

Something similar has happened to civil rights organizations in America. After worthy goals such as school desegregation had been accomplished, civil rights groups set other goals, such as expanding affirmative action programs. As time went by, each successive goal became less significant and bore less resemblance to the original goals of the organization.

Eventually, after the Civil Rights Movement had made significant progress in eliminating individual racism, in order to remain relevant it had to create new forms of racism to eradicate—hence, concepts like "institutional racism."

For example, a congresswoman from Houston, Texas, once complained that too few hurricanes were named after black people. Of course, when this hypersensitive member of the Congressional Black Caucus made her claim, she was not really accusing meteorologists at the National Hurricane Center of operating out of a belief in the genetic inferiority of certain races. She was just claiming that the process of naming hurricanes tended to exclude African Americans disproportionately. In other words, she was claiming institutional racism—although most thought she was just blowing gale-force hot air.

But you know what's interesting? No civil rights leader has ever claimed that our Social Security system is a form of institutional racism. And yet, according to the definition of "institutional racism," Social Security is a deeply racist institution.

Everyone who works pays into the Social Security system through a lifetime of "contributions," which are actually forcibly extracted by the government. But no one is allowed to draw full benefits until they turn sixty-five years of age. This is racially biased because white Americans have a greater life expectancy than black Americans—and an especially greater life expectancy than black men, who live, on average, shorter lives, while black women, white men, and white women all can expect to live past seventy years of age.

To make matters worse, the solvency of Social Security is in jeopardy. The result is that Congress will soon have to move the age of eligibility for full Social Security benefits to seventy years. This means that every demographic group within the population will be paying into the Social Security system, and everyone except the average black male will draw out.

Put simply, African American men are working all their lives to contribute to a system from which the average black man will never benefit. On top of that, he is not able to pass his contributions on to his offspring when he dies. Instead, the money—not just a simple majority of it but also a disproportionate share—will go toward creating a secure retirement for white people.

This could be compared to working on a plantation. The black man works, but the white man gets to keep the proceeds of the labor.

The Social Security system was established in 1935 by FDR. It was followed by a mass shift of African Americans to the Democratic Party. They had previously avoided the Democratic Party because the Republican Party was seen as more sympathetic to their plight as slaves.

But when FDR came along with the New Deal, which included Social Security, black voters returned to the Democratic Party. They thought FDR was more sympathetic to the poorer classes who were disproportionately black. Since then, African Americans have continued to vote Democratic.

And, since then, no one seems to have discussed that strange paradox—at least not in the mainstream media.

The old form of slavery motivated by the old form of racism drove black voters away from the Democratic Party. A new form of slavery that perfectly fits the definition of a new form of racism drove them back. The truth is often stranger than fiction. But it's the only thing that will set men free.

Roger Bannister and the Twenty-Five-Year Mile

Zach,

I assume you have heard of a man named Roger Bannister. Back in 1954, he did something everyone said was impossible. He ran a mile in under four minutes—breaking the barrier by only six-tenths of a second. No one in all of recorded human history had ever run a mile in less than four minutes. But soon afterwards (just forty-six days later), a man named John Landy broke Bannister's record.

To date, it appears that well over 1,000 different people—perhaps 1,100, according to some sources—have recorded a sub-four-minute mile. In fact, no official consensus on the exact number seems to exist now that so many people have done it so often. The discrepancy between what was once thought impossible and what has now been achieved has implications for the current debate over affirmative action.

When we raise the bar for human achievement in any particular arena, human beings rise to the occasion. When we lower the bar, human beings simply exert less effort. Unfortunately, lowering the bar for human achievement is precisely what affirmative action does. My friend Larry Purdy, who served as trial counsel in the famous *Grutter v. Bollinger* case, said it best: "Those to whom a lower standard is applied cannot possibly grow to their full height."

If Larry Purdy is right, we have cause for great concern. Justice Sandra Day O'Connor spoke for the 5–4 majority in *Grutter* when she said, "We expect that 25 years from now, the use of racial preferences will no longer be necessary to further the interest approved today."

The "interest" to which Justice O'Connor referred is called "diversity." She assumes that racial preferences are needed to create racial diversity. But consider the following:

- The state of Washington outlawed racial preferences in a voter initiative passed in 1998. In the fall of 1998, when race was still being considered in students' applications, the flagship school University of Washington had 124 African Americans enrolled in its freshman class.

The year after the initiative passed, black enrollment dropped dramatically. But the following year black enrollment rebounded back to 119.

- In the fall of 1996, when race was still being used to grant admissions to the University of Texas at Austin, 4.1 percent of the incoming freshman class was black. By the fall of 1999, Texas was using a system that did not take account of race—instead admitting the top 10 percent from every Texas high school regardless of race. In that year, 4.1 percent of the incoming freshman class at the University of Texas at Austin was black. Another stunning comeback was achieved.

- In the fall of 2004, Texas A&M University had a combined black/Hispanic enrollment of 15 percent without taking race into account in admissions. The University of Michigan, still relying on the race-based system it successfully defended in *Grutter v. Bollinger* in 2003, had a combined black/Hispanic enrollment of just 12 percent in the fall of 2004.

The data from Washington support my twofold contention that a) lowering the bar for African Americans, or any other race, results in lower performance, and b) raising the bar for black students, or those of any race, results in higher performance. In this case, black high school students responded positively and quickly to the higher demands placed upon them.

The data from Texas support my argument that diversity, even racial diversity, doesn't need to be established and preserved by race-based admissions. Why then do university administrators defend racial preferences?

It is important to understand that college presidents often work within larger university systems. For example, my university is just one of seventeen in the larger UNC system. Our chancellor would be rightfully concerned that eliminating race preferences for admissions to our campus immediately and unilaterally would cause UNC-Wilmington to lose black applicants to other schools in the UNC system.

Schools such as UNC-Greensboro and UNC-Asheville, for example, would like to see UNC-Wilmington make just such a unilateral change. They would clearly benefit.

Therefore, it is not realistic to expect our university administrators to take the lead by instituting changes at their individual universities. Real change can only come from making sweeping changes across entire public university systems. That has been done in states such as Texas and Washington, and you've just read about the results.

Zach, in a conversation during my office hours last semester you voiced your support for race-based affirmative action. You talked about how easy it had been to grow up white instead of black. You argued that affirmative action is what "we" owe to "them."

But "we" don't owe anyone a system that keeps "them" down. Instead, we need a system that promotes high achievement for everyone—and closes the gap between "us" and "them."

Put simply, Zach, if you support affirmative action, you cannot continue to call yourself "progressive." It would be more accurate to call yourself "regressive" instead.

The Unholy Trinity of Diversity

Dear Zach,

I'd like to tell you the story of a revealing incident in the history of race relations, "diversity," and free speech on the American college campus.

It occurred back in the spring of 1992 on the campus of Mississippi State University (MSU). The student newspaper published a cartoon that was meant to poke fun at the hypocrisy of white racists. The cartoon pictured a white racist sitting back in his chair complaining about the laziness of black people. The language he was using made not only his racism but also his generally low level of education

29

crystal clear. This character was surrounded by trash and empty beer cans while denigrating African Americans for allegedly living like pigs.

To anyone—especially, anyone who had ever seen the TV show *All in the Family*—the intent of the author of the cartoon was obvious. He was trying to send a message of disapproval of white racism by making fun of white racists.

But many black students on the MSU campus saw it differently, claiming the cartoon offended them. So they gathered by the scores in front of the Colvard Student Union in order to protest. It should go without saying that they looked very silly protesting a cartoon that was meant to attack white racist hypocrisy.

When the subject of the protest came up in a meeting at the Social Science Research Center, a professor defended the protestors saying, "You have to understand that racial tensions are high on campus these days." But they should not have been high. If anything, they should have been lower than ever. Let me explain with a brief historical digression.

In 1965, the year my father graduated from MSU, the school finally got around to admitting its first black student. Less than a quarter of a century later, in 1989 to be exact, the university elected its first black Student Government Association (SGA) president, Steven Cooper. Remarkably, we elected our second black SGA president, Kelvin Covington, the very next year.

So how are we to interpret the professor's exhortation that we needed to "understand that racial tensions are high on campus these days" when "these days" referred to the aftermath of significant civil rights gains for African Americans on campus? The answer is that the "days" to which he was referring were the early 1990s. That was when campus speech codes were introduced to most institutions of higher learning in America.

Do you recall "effort justification"? After the Civil Rights Movement accomplished its major goals, it moved on to smaller and, frankly, less worthy aims. One of those new goals was ensuring that black people felt comfortable at all times. That is how we got campus speech codes.

But those speech codes were not exclusively for black students—at least not for very long. Within a few years, they became a major cause of the campus feminist movement. That fact is unsurprising given that the Anita Hill/Clarence Thomas fiasco roughly corresponds to this time period.

Before the Thomas confirmation hearings, the term "sexual harassment" was generally restricted to *quid pro quo* harassment—a situation in which a woman was coerced into sexual relations in exchange for keeping her job or procuring a promotion. But after the Thomas confirmation hearings, campus authorities began to take a greater interest in so-called "hostile environment" sexual harassment.

Speech codes were seen as a major way of preventing "hostile environment" harassment. The fusion of speech codes with anti-harassment efforts is reflected in our university's current harassment definition, which reads,

> *Harassment is unwelcome conduct based on race, color, religion, creed, sex, national origin, age, disability, veteran status or sexual orientation that is either a condition of working or learning (quid pro quo) or creates a hostile environment.*

It should not take much time to discern two serious problems with this exceedingly vague definition of harassment. First of all, it makes no distinction between verbal and non-verbal conduct. Second, it does not include any requirement that the conduct in question be repeated in order to constitute "harassment." A harassment charge could result from a single instance of verbal conduct that creates a so-called hostile environment. In other words, a person could be charged for simply saying something that makes someone feel uncomfortable on a single occasion.

That is not merely a matter of speculation. It is, in fact, what has happened on more than one occasion at UNC-Wilmington. A couple of actual examples:

- A professor in the political science department was accused of sexual harassment for calling a female student "honey." The student was administering first aid after the professor had sprained an ankle. He was directing her to the source of a physical injury. He was hardly in a position or state of mind to make a real sexual advance. Thankfully, the charges were later dismissed.

- A philosophy professor went to her dean with a sexual harassment complaint about another philosophy professor. Her allegation was that the professor had argued that some rapes are worse than others, and that therefore there should be more than one degree of rape in the criminal rape statutes. It is worth noting that this is, in fact, the current law in most states. Nonetheless, the professor accused her colleague of sexual harassment because she felt (emphasis on "felt") that he was saying that some rapes were not serious, which she felt (more emphasis on "felt") created a hostile environment.

More recently, campus speech codes have been used to remove protection from speech seen as "homophobic" by gay rights activists. An illustrative and enlightening example of this trend occurred on our campus just a couple of years ago. One UNCW student wrote the word "fag" on the apartment door of another UNCW student. Despite the fact that the incident occurred off campus, UNCW authorities investigated it.

When it was discovered that the incident was nothing more than a stupid joke between friends—notably, a joke between two heterosexual friends—the matter was dropped.

But that was not enough to satisfy a gay male secretary who worked on campus. He continued lobbying to have the incident classified as the "hate crime" of homophobic "hate speech." He even contacted the county civil rights office in order to re-open the investigation. Thankfully, his efforts failed.

Zach, I am thankful when such cases fail for one very important reason. Such cases always cause harm to the groups they seek to help. In other words, they bring down the very groups they seek to elevate.

White racists have always seen African Americans as hypersensitive and volatile. To the extent that we use speech codes to try to protect black people from ever being offended, we reinforce that stereotype. (Not to mention that the notion that we can use speech codes to protect black students from being "offended" and simultaneously hire performers such as Ludacris and Kanye West, rappers famous for lyrics including words like "n——r" and "b—-h," to sing on campus is obviously deeply hypocritical. I am referring to our decisions to hire Ludacris and West to perform on our campus a few years ago.)

This same line of reasoning is similarly applicable in the case of women. Sexists have always seen women as hypersensitive and emotionally volatile. To the extent that we use speech codes to try to protect them from ever being offended, we reinforce that stereotype. (The notion that we can sponsor feminist plays featuring words like "c—t" and simultaneously protect women from being "offended" is also deeply hypocritical. I am referring to our decision to sponsor *The Vagina Monologues* every year.)

And, finally, in the case of homosexuals, the same reasoning still applies. Their critics have always seen gay people as hypersensitive and emotionally volatile. To the extent that we use speech codes to try to protect them from being offended, we reinforce that stereotype.

Progressives do not have an agenda that resonates with a majority of the people. Hence, if they want to effect real political change, they must get various victim groups to join together in forming these kinds of coalitions. Much of what the victims' coalition promotes goes under the name of "diversity," but what it really boils down is to a kind of cultural Marxism. And the only thing these "diverse" groups really have in common is that they are equally harmed by the condescending hypocrisy of the authors of campus speech codes.

Plus, there is one especially good reason why two of the three parts of the unholy trinity of diversity should not be joined together. I call the trinity "unholy" because, quite literally, one of these groups is killing off another with its principal public-policy position. Feminists work tirelessly to keep abortion legal, while about half of all unborn black babies are aborted. Talk about "institutional racism."

Explaining Unexplained Variance

Zach,

It is time for me to speak very directly about one of the main reasons why I no longer consider myself to be a progressive—and why I am urging you to reconsider your commitment to progressive politics. I am speaking here of the substantial setbacks in race relations that progressives in the social sciences have caused. These pseudo-scholars have amassed volumes of pseudo-scientific literature that does more than simply exaggerate the amount of racial discrimination in modern day America. It actually invents the patterns out of whole cloth. Sadly,

few offenders have been worse than contemporary criminologists—many of whom received their training in departments of sociology.

One of the worst examples of illusory racism I have seen
comes from a book called *Race and Criminal Justice*, edited
by Michael Lynch and Britt Patterson. In several chapters
of the book, the authors ably demonstrate that it is easy to
present an illusion of racism where none exists by using
statistical manipulations that few people understand. Their
chapter on racial disparity in bail allotment is particularly
disturbing in this regard.

Before I proceed, I need to explain why it is so important
to employ careful statistical controls when studying racial
disparity in the criminal justice system. Let me use a brief
illustration within the context of sentencing.

Imagine that you have a prison located in the Mississippi Delta—an area that is notorious for its history of racism. Within that prison you draw a sample of 100 black and
100 white prisoners. You then calculate average sentences
for each racial group. Your results indicate that the average
sentence for a black inmate is 15.5 years while the average
sentence for a white inmate is 12.3 years. Do you conclude
that racism accounts for the 3.2-year difference in incarceration length between blacks and whites?

Of course you should do no such thing! Not if you call
yourself a scientist. You have not yet accounted for other
variables that may explain part or all of the difference in

average sentence length. In other words, you have not entered all of the appropriate statistical controls into the equation.

Next, imagine that you do control for two obvious factors that are always relevant at sentencing—offense severity and prior record. Your hypothetical study now finds that the black inmates were committing slightly more serious offenses and had slightly longer rap sheets prior to incarceration on their current offense. Therefore, the statistically controlled sentencing difference drops to 2.2 years of incarceration. Do you now conclude that racism accounts for the difference in incarceration length between blacks and whites? Not yet.

Finally, I want you to imagine that there are three more variables that can legitimately be used in sentencing. You next enter these factors as statistical controls in your study. Now you find that the sentencing difference drops down to 1.5 years of disparity between those same 100 blacks and 100 whites in the prison study. You are now likely to conclude that racial discrimination costs the average black prisoner 1.5 years of his personal liberty. But not so fast.

That 1.5-year difference between blacks and whites is called "unexplained variance." Once they have exhausted all explanations arising from the severity of the crime and the laws governing sentencing, researchers who study race in sentencing routinely assume that the remaining difference is due to race. After all, no other legitimate factor seems to explain the variance. But such an assumption might not be warranted. It is entirely possible that the unexplained variance could be due to social class or some other variable that simply was not measured in the study.

But what would we think if the researchers in a race study of this kind had failed to control for even all of the legitimate sentencing factors—and still claimed that the unexplained variance was due to race? Of course, such a claim should not be taken seriously.

Enter Lynch and Patterson. In the bail allotment study they published in *Race and Criminal Justice,* the original researchers failed to control for all of the factors that can be used in sentencing. In fact, they simply omitted several important legal variables from their study. Nonetheless, the researchers claimed that the bail allotment disparity demonstrated racism simply because they found race differences (such as whites getting lower bail, on average) that were not explained by the variables they did include in their study. It bears repeating—they made this claim even though they failed to measure all of the legal variables that judges are supposed to use when setting bail.

In other words, they had no difficulty getting someone to publish a study making unwarranted accusations of racism against criminal justice professionals. Unfortunately, it gets even worse than that.

In another chapter, Lynch and Patterson's book includes the same egregious error again—this time in the context of race and the death penalty. This skewed study, conducted by a University of Central Florida criminologist named Robert Bohm, goes even further—actually making false claims of genocide on the basis of crude models lacking simple statistical controls.

In his study, Bohm examines differences in the relative frequency of black and white executions before and after the seminal Supreme Court case of *Furman v. Georgia*, decided in 1972.

Zach, as you recall from taking my criminal justice class, the Furman case involved a black man named Willie Furman, who was convicted of killing a white man. After he was sentenced to die, Furman appealed to the Supreme Court, claiming that Georgia death penalty statutes were rigged in such a way that it was virtually impossible for a white man to be sentenced to die for killing a black man. In contrast, he claimed, it was not just likely but indeed probable that a black man would be sentenced to die for the premeditated murder of a white man. The Furman case was one that involved real evidence of racism.

The result of the case was a moratorium on executions in the United States that lasted for five years. After the case, states modified their sentencing statutes to reduce racial disparity in executions. After executions resumed, many criminologists began examining executions to see whether those legal modifications had worked to iron racism out of capital punishment. Professor Bohm published his study in *Race and Criminal Justice* after several hundred post-Furman executions had been carried out. Unsurprisingly, he claimed evidence of continued racism in executions.

As evidence of continued racism, Professor Bohm cited the fact that nearly half of those executed since Furman have been black, while African Americans constitute only about 12 percent of the population. What Bohm had obviously failed to emphasize—or, apparently, even consider—is that most homicides are committed by African Americans despite the fact that they constitute only 12 percent of the population of the United States. As of this writing, statistics indicate that blacks commit about 53 percent of all criminal homicides in the U.S.

In other words, Professor Bohm perpetuates the myth of racism in the death penalty by failing to account for even the most basic of statistical controls—actual criminal behavior. This would amount to professional malpractice if only criminology were considered to be a serious profession. Fortunately, Professor Bohm's studies are not widely read by the public. But they are assigned to college students in their sociology and criminology classes, with two unfortunate results:

1. They motivate some students to dedicate their professional lives to finding solutions to nonexistent problems.

2. They cause many students to become angry over things that aren't even true.

I have written this letter—indeed, this series of letters—to you in the hope that you will not get stuck in the second of those two traps. Life is too short to spend being angry about things that aren't even true. Most of your professors fail to understand that. They think they're working to overturn false criminal convictions, but really many criminologists are fostering false personal convictions about race and other important matters. In the process, they sentence their students to a life of self-righteous anger with little chance of parole.

Author's note: As of this writing, 18 million black babies have been aborted since the Furman case. Not one of them has committed a crime. None has been afforded due process. Professor Bohm has remained mute on that issue. Instead, he continues to claim that the execution of hundreds of black murderers over a span of several decades is an effort to control the black population by "extermination or threat of extermination." During the same time frame, slightly more than half of those executed have been white. Meanwhile, as I pointed out in my last letter, approximately half of all black pregnancies end in abortion.

How to Slay Goliath with Just One Stone

Dear Zach,

Abortion is *the* issue where all the progressives' noblest claims—to be fighting for racial equality, to care sincerely about the weakest among us, to have beliefs grounded in reason and science—are shown up for the sham they really are.

Whenever I end up in an extended argument about abortion, I find that there are about six points I can expect to encounter before the argument has come to term, so to speak. But, fortunately, the six arguments all suffer from one fatal flaw, which makes them somewhat easy to rebut as long as the proponent of life stays focused on the central question of the abortion debate: "Are the unborn human?"

I've listed the six arguments below—along with specific common-sense rebuttals to each.

Zach, this issue is really the most obvious weak point of the progressive outlook that you've adopted at college. Here's where it becomes crystal clear that the conservative Christians you've come to despise are actually the ones on the right side of history—and that they have reason and science on their side, too. And I know that the abortion issue is the weak point in your own personal progressive armor—I've noticed that it's the one issue where you haven't been willing to defend progressive views against un-"enlightened" conservative Christian opinion. So I urge you to consider these arguments, and to reconsider the question of who really wishes to defend the weakest among us, and who wishes to deny their humanity:

1. "It's my body, my choice."

This argument is extremely easy to dismantle because the unborn baby has its own distinct genetic code, which is generating growth from conception. Not only is there unique DNA, but also in 100 percent of abortions the baby already has a detectable heartbeat. Doctors will not even perform abortions until six or seven weeks into the pregnancy—in order to protect the health of the mother. The doctor wants to be able to account for and remove all of the baby's body parts because if some small portion of the baby remains in the mother's body, it could cause a deadly infection. The irony is lost on most of these so-called health-care professionals.

So the woman who says "my body, my choice" is in the absurd position of arguing that she has two noses, four legs, two brains, and two skeletal systems. This kind of absurdity requires no further elaboration. It is nothing more than feminist foot-stomping to assert the "my body, my choice" argument, a kind of "mine, mine" argument that is unbecoming from anyone over the age of two.

2. "Back-alley abortions will increase if abortion is illegal."

This argument, like the first, simply assumes that the unborn are not persons. If they were persons, then the abortion choice advocate would be in the awkward position of arguing that someone has a right to commit murder in a safe and sterile environment. This hardly survives the straight-face test. But if for some reason your opponent can't see its absurdity, tell him the following: "I'm planning to rob the Wells Fargo Bank across the street but there is ice all over the sidewalk. I'm afraid I might slip and fall during my escape. Could you call them and tell them to salt the sidewalk before I commit the robbery? And hurry up. I need the cash!"

Proponents of this argument often quote appalling statistics—that when abortion was illegal 10,000 women per year died using coat-hangers on themselves in back alleys. But those numbers are both false and irrelevant. Within a few years after abortion was made a constitutional right, the number of abortions skyrocketed. Over a million more babies were being killed per year within just a few years after *Roe v. Wade*. The fact that they were killed in a sterile, well-lit environment did not make them any less dead. Please review argument #1.

3. "It is wrong to force a woman to bring an unwanted baby into the world."

Put simply, there is no such thing as an "unwanted baby." If a baby is unwanted by its mother, there is always, and I mean always, someone else who would want to adopt the baby. It is very difficult to adopt a baby in this country because so many children are unnecessarily aborted. But there is something even more sick and twisted about the "unwanted baby" excuse—it insinuates that abortion prevents child abuse. But abortion *is* child abuse—the most severe kind, where the baby ends up dead. Please review argument #1 before reading further.

The very idea that we would murder children to prevent child abuse, which usually takes the form of simple battery, elevates intellectual laziness to an art. It is the intellectual equivalent of promoting arson in order to prevent burglary. It is true that burglary rates will decrease when we have burned down everyone's houses, but by now you get the point.

Finally, it is worth mentioning that abortion has not been an effective means of stopping child abuse (even if we exclude abortion from the definition of child abuse). In 1973, there were 167,000 reported instances of child abuse. By 1982, reported instances of child abuse had risen to 929,000. That is an increase of over 500 percent in less than a decade. When will liberals take responsibility for this unmitigated disaster?

4. "It is wrong for a woman to be forced to bring a handicapped baby into the world."

It is frequently suggested that abortion is morally permissible when doctors discover, prior to birth, that a baby suffers from certain physical handicaps such as Down syndrome or cerebral palsy. My response usually goes something like this:

"I agree that there are far too many handicapped people in the world. Every summer I take busloads of people who are wheelchair-bound on a trip to the Grand Canyon. We enjoy the view for a few minutes before I roll them off the edge of the Canyon. They are usually dead long before they hit the bottom. That is a good thing for them and for society as a whole. It is better to be dead than to be handicapped. Whether they realize it or not, their lives are not worth living."

This scenario provokes a strong reaction—as it should. Something about it makes advocates of aborting the handicapped look grossly insensitive. This is usually when they argue that they are not killing a handicapped person but rather preventing a handicapped person from ever being born. Please review argument #1.

The last time I spoke on this topic at Summit Ministries, a handsome, intelligent, and athletic 6'2" African American student approached me and told me, "I was misdiagnosed with cerebral palsy before I was born. The doctors were wrong. I am so glad my mother had me. Thank you for your speech."

5. "It is wrong for a woman to be forced to give birth to a baby she cannot afford."

This argument is also remarkably callous—so much so that it is difficult to understand how those who make it could describe themselves as "liberal." Do we really need to start reassigning Jonathan Swift's *Modest Proposal* to underline how profoundly sick and distasteful this argument really is? Swift wrote—satirically, of course—a proposal that suggested people eat their babies in order to relieve their hunger and poverty. Serious arguments in favor of "choice" often sound chillingly similar.

For those who have never read Swift, I like to point to a more contemporary example. In the 80s, a punk rock band called The Dead Kennedys wrote a song called "Kill the Poor" in which they mockingly suggested that we kill poor people as a means of eliminating poverty. That would certainly eliminate poverty. But is it really an acceptable solution? Of course not. That was their point.

It's a good idea to confront the advocates of legal abortion with the question of whether it is permissible to kill to eliminate poverty. In response, they typically say something like this: "No, I would never advocate killing the poor. I would advocate abortion to prevent them from becoming poor people in the first place." They are trapped once again in the untenable position of denying the personhood of the unborn. Please review argument #1.

Of course, there is another aspect to the poverty-as-a-defense-of-abortion argument. It is the crass argument that the mother cannot "afford" the baby. This raises another fundamental question: "Is it permissible to kill a person in order to alleviate financial stress?" If so, I'd like to kill the banker who holds my mortgage. Just kidding. Of course, I cannot do that anyway since a) he is a middle-aged man and b) the Supreme Court does not authorize abortions in the 200th trimester—at least, they haven't yet!

6. "It is wrong to force a woman to give birth to a baby after she has been a victim of rape (or incest, which is almost always statutory rape)."

Whenever I hear an argument for the rape exception, I think of my friend Laura. She was adopted, and in her twenties she wanted to locate her birth mother and learn about the circumstances of her adoption. When she did, she found out that she was the product of a rape. I don't have the audacity to tell her an abortionist should have killed her. I leave that to the compassionate liberals who oversimplify the rape issue.

Actually, "oversimplify" is too kind a term. They are exploiting the rape issue in order to avoid the central question of the debate: "Is the unborn child—yes, even the product of a rape—human?" I say, "Of course!" And Laura agrees with me. If you disagree, then you may take it up with her or with others conceived in rape, such as attorney and pro-life advocate Rebecca Kiessling. Their lives are hardly useless. And because their mothers had the courage to bear them, they have made a profound difference in this world—including saving countless lives with their pro-life testimony.

Whenever the issue of the rape exception is raised, it is well worth mentioning *Kennedy v. Louisiana,* decided by the Supreme Court in 2008. The Court spared Kennedy from execution on the grounds that it would be "cruel and unusual punishment" to execute a man who had not killed anyone. This was a brutal rape case—indeed, among the worst I've ever studied. An expert in pediatric forensic medicine testified at Kennedy's trial that Kennedy had raped his eight-year-old stepdaughter savagely, to the point of causing permanent physical damage. In fact, a laceration to the left wall of her vagina had separated her cervix from the back of her vagina and caused her rectum to protrude into her vaginal structure. Put simply, Kennedy raped, sodomized, and viciously tortured the little girl. Thankfully, he was easily convicted for doing so. There is no question whatsoever about his guilt.

But the high court ruled that Kennedy's execution would violate the Eighth Amendment because of "evolving standards of decency that mark the progress of a maturing society." This decision rested largely on the fact that most states reject the idea of execution for rape—even the rape of a young child, even accompanied by other aggravating factors. As a result, this is the position in which we find ourselves: When a woman is raped she has a constitutional right to an abortion. And the rapist has a constitutional right to life. But the unborn baby has no rights whatsoever.

The Kennedy case helps us to better understand another frequently employed argument for the rape exception—that a woman has a right to abort in order to rid her of the memory of a horrible event. But this argument is both logically and factually flawed.

Logically speaking, the woman, if granted the right to kill one person, should be entitled to kill the rapist. She should not be entitled to kill the baby! Any assertion to the contrary can be justified only by denying the personhood of the unborn. Once again, review argument #1.

Factually speaking, there is simply no merit to the argument that abortions either soothe the conscience or assuage the memory of rape victims. In the first place, too many women feel guilty and blame themselves in the aftermath of rape, and getting an abortion adds another layer of guilt and trauma. Only the birth of the child can provide healing—even if the child is immediately given up for adoption. Philosophers since Socrates have been pointing out that it is better to suffer evil than to inflict it. Planned Parenthood counselors are never inclined to raise this point. They profit from the infliction of evil upon the innocent. And they use rape victims to justify their occupation.

After I have finished making all the points I wish to make, I always extend the following offer to my opponent: "If I agree to write in the exception for rape, will you be willing to lobby for the law banning all other abortions?" In all of my years discussing abortion, no one has taken me up on the offer. Their reaction always shows that they were never in favor of keeping abortion legal in order to protect victims of rape. They are simply using these women for political purposes.

Zach, a movement that both denies the personhood of the defenseless unborn and uses rape victims for political purposes is not one worth belonging to.

Trading Live Babies for Government Programs

Zach,

Welcome back to campus. I hope the beginning of the fall semester is going well for you. Thank you for coming by my office during registration last week. It was good to see you, and even better to hear your thoughts on the points I made about abortion in my last letter. I'm impressed by your open-minded attitude on the issue, and I appreciate your interest in continuing our discussion of that and related issues during this academic year.

Recently, a former university student sent me a video of a speech I gave on abortion a few years ago. Any speech

given on a liberal university campus is likely to be contentious, given that many schools have a history of allowing
protestors to shout down speakers with whom they disagree. But because my speech was on abortion, it was particularly contentious.

After the speech, which took place at the University of
Massachusetts at Amherst, was over, we had a Q&A session
that was tame by comparison. In fact, it was slightly boring.
The only highlight of the session was my exchange with a
graduate student. Below, I have reproduced the exchange
to the best of my ability:

Student: In your speech, you say that you are
opposed to abortion under virtually every cir-
cumstance. If you are not willing to preserve the
legality of abortion then I was just wondering
whether you would support any of the following
programs, which would ease the repercussions of
making abortion illegal. For example, would you
support national health care in order to provide
medical check-ups for women? Also, would you
support a national daycare program for those
who cannot afford to stay home with their babies?
As an educator, you know the importance of education. So I am wondering if you would support
additional sex education programs in our public
school system. And, since not everyone goes to

school, would you support publicly funded sex education classes for adults?

Me: Ma'am.

Student: I'm not finished yet.

Me: I know you aren't finished, but most people just ask one question and you are firing off a number of them. I think I can save you some time by answering all of your questions with one simple answer: No, I would not.

Student: Why aren't you willing to support any of these measures?

Me: Because each one includes either the word "national" or the word "public."

Student: I don't understand.

Me: Well, put simply, each time you use the word "national" you are referring to the national government. Each time you use the word "public" you are referring to the local government. Either way, you are suggesting you will drop your support for abortion in exchange for more government

spending. Now let me ask you a question. Are you
a graduate student?

Student: I am.

Me: What is your major?

Student: Public Policy and Administration.

At this point in the exchange, the student tried to shout
more questions out as I spoke to her. So I moved on to the
next student. But had I been able to stop her barrage of
questions, I would have ended the exchange this way:

Me: Well, there we have it. All of the government
programs you recommend would be run by people with Masters in Public Administration, or
MPA, degrees. What you are really asking me is
whether I would be willing to trade government
jobs for live babies. I think that is truly shameful.
I am here to help save lives, not to help grow the
government. And if you concede that abortion
takes life, then you should oppose it without any
further financial incentive.

The exchange suggested to me that some feminists would
be willing to drop their support of abortion rights if it meant

they could profit from it by securing more government jobs. This could cause tension within the feminist movement, especially given that so many people are already profiting financially from the abortion trade. That will be the subject of our next correspondence.

LETTER 10

Blood Money

Zach,

Let me quote you some disturbing statistics about the abortion industry. According to the website Abort73.com,

> The Alan Guttmacher Institute (AGI), the research arm of Planned Parenthood, estimates that there were 1.21 million abortions performed in the U.S. in the year 2005. Of the 1.21 million annual abortions, approximately 88% (1.06 million) are performed during the first

trimester. The other 12% (150,000) are performed during the second and third trimester. In 2005, the average cost of a nonhospital abortion with local anesthesia at 10 weeks of gestation was $413. The Women's Medical Center estimates that a 2nd trimester abortion costs up to $3000 (with the price increasing the further along the pregnancy goes). If we take the $413 average for 1st trimester abortions and use a $3000 average for 2nd and 3rd trimester abortions, here's what we get: $438 million is spent each year on first trimester abortions and $393 million is spent on late term abortions. That means that each year in the U.S., the abortion industry brings in approximately $831 million through their abortion services alone. If you add in the $337 million (or more) that Planned Parenthood (America's largest abortion provider) receives annually in government grants and contracts, the annual dollar amount moves well past 1 billion.

Abortion, to put it plainly, is a very lucrative business, and this has been true from the beginning. By last count, Planned Parenthood (a tax-exempt organization!) has $951 million in total assets!

In addition to organizations, there are also a lot of individual doctors getting rich off of abortion. In his now-classic book, *Pro-life Answers to Pro-choice Arguments*, Randy Alcorn points out, "In 1992, when the average annual income for a physician in Portland, Oregon, was just under $100,000, a local abortionist testified in court that in the previous year his income had been $345,000. One physician says, 'an abortionist, working only twenty or thirty hours a week, with no overhead, can earn from three to ten times as much as an ethical surgeon.'" Abortion has been a very lucrative business for a very long time.

And, sadly, one of the reasons performing abortions is so lucrative is that abortionists are less likely to be sued for malpractice. No matter how badly some women are hurt, they do not want to reveal the fact that they have had abortions. So they stay out of court. And therefore the abortionists stay out of trouble.

The facts about the profitability of the abortion industry may help us to understand a few things about feminist resistance to free speech specifically, and to the free flow of information generally:

1. **Crisis Pregnancy Centers (CPCs).** It has been ten years since we at UNC-Wilmington established a Women's Resource Center (WRC). For nine of those ten years, I have been trying to get

our local crisis pregnancy center linked on the WRC website, which is hosted by our university. But the feminists who maintain the WRC website have refused to include the link, claiming that they don't have room on the website for both Planned Parenthood and the CPC. They have also said they cannot include the CPC because it is "overtly religious." But most feminist criticisms of CPCs have not centered on religion specifically. Instead, they have centered on the more general accusation that CPCs try to make women feel guilty if they are even considering an abortion. These critics sometimes say that the real motivation for showing ultrasound images of the unborn baby is to make the woman "emotional" in order to get her to avoid making the "rational decision" to abort.

But all of these explanations gloss over the fact that CPCs cost the abortion industry money. And money is a big reason why Planned Parenthood and its feminist allies would like to keep abortion safe, legal—and frequent. If Planned Parenthood is a pregnant woman's only source of counseling, then the chance she will keep her baby is only about 10 percent. By contrast, some CPCs claim that by offering alternative counseling they can increase the chances that a woman will keep her baby to about 50 percent. And if the CPC is equipped with ultrasound technology (and the woman sees her unborn baby via sonogram), then the chance she will have her baby actually skyrockets to around 90 percent.

2. **Breast Cancer Awareness.** When I first heard that abortions significantly increase a woman's chances of getting breast cancer, I was confused. I simply didn't get the connection. But upon further reflection, it makes perfect sense. When a woman gets pregnant she experiences a rapid growth of breast tissue. An abortion creates an unnatural condition since the woman's breast tissue is growing to prepare for a baby that is no longer there. That is the reason why women who have first trimester abortions double their chances of getting breast cancer. Professor Joel Brind of City University of New York has written a comprehensive study of the subject called *Review and Meta-Analysis of the Abortion/ Breast Cancer Link.* Here's what he has to say about the level of cancer risk brought about by abortion: "The single most avoidable risk factor for breast cancer is induced abortion."

Now, ask yourself a question, Zach. In all the years that our university has sponsored breast cancer awareness seminars and speeches, have you ever heard a discussion of the issue of abortion? Clearly, discussing the role abortion plays in breast cancer poses a risk to those who profit from providing abortions. And so the information is routinely suppressed. If you don't believe me, then just do a quick Google search of our university website. Nowhere—not in any course syllabus or any other published document—is the link between breast cancer and abortion mentioned. Nor is any professor at our university (besides me) currently discussing or researching the issue. It is simply dumbfounding.

3. **Parental Notification Laws.** In addition to preventing free speech on a wide range of issues like abortion and breast cancer, feminists often try to prevent the free flow of information between private parties—where there is a chance that the information might reduce the number of abortions. A prime example of this phenomenon is the staunch feminist opposition to parental notification laws. When a twelve-year-old girl becomes pregnant, there is little sense arguing that she has the maturity to understand the consequences of an abortion. Indeed, there is little chance that she

understood the consequences of sex in the first place—hence the unexpected pregnancy. So she really should talk to one or both parents before having an abortion. Nonetheless, the feminist movement fights tooth and nail against parental notification laws because there is a very good chance that parents will be opposed to their little twelve-year-old getting an abortion. And, as we discussed previously, such opposition would cut into the profits of the abortion industry.

So now we find ourselves in a strange place in America. If a teenager wants an abortion, she can have it. But if sometime later on she becomes upset and cries hard enough to get a headache and she needs an aspirin, then she's out of luck. The school nurse can't give her an aspirin without first securing parental permission. Abortion "yes," but aspirin "no." Which one would you say is more likely to be harmful to a twelve-year-old?

4. **Reporting Statutory Rape.** Over the course of the last several years, numerous undercover sting operations have caused Planned Parenthood great embarrassment. In some of the operations, young women have called a Planned Parenthood clinic to report that they

were pregnant—specifically identifying themselves as under the age of consent. In recorded phone calls, Planned Parenthood employees make it clear that they are willing to provide abortions—without reporting the statutory rapes. Recordings of some of these phone conversations have been released to the media, causing great embarrassment to the "prochoice" movement. After several of these sting operations were conducted over the phone, some pro-life organizations decided to start conducting them in person using hidden cameras.

In June of 2008, two college women volunteering for Students for Life of America (SFLA) entered two clinics in North Carolina posing as underage girls. One posed as a fifteen-year-old, and the other posed as a fourteen-year-old. Both claimed they had just had unprotected sex with their mother's boyfriend, who was in his thirties. Each girl also told the clinic workers that the boyfriend had suggested that she come get the "morning after" pill. According to North Carolina law, this information is enough to trigger mandatory statutory rape reporting. In other words, anyone aware of such information must report it to proper state or local authorities.

In both visits, staffers acknowledged that what was happening to the girls was, in fact, statutory rape. In North Carolina, the age of consent is sixteen and the perpetrator only needs to be four years older than the victim. Of course, all of the staffers were aware of the law—and in one case a staffer repeatedly admitted that they were required to report the incident.

After the visits, SFLA filed two North Carolina Public Records Requests (under N.C.G.S. Section 132) in order to find out if the Planned Parenthood locations had reported the crimes. SFLA obtained and posted online documents showing that the crimes were not reported to authorities in either Charlotte or Winston-Salem—the respective locations of the two clinics where the sting operations occurred.

This is chilling when you stop to think about it. For years, the abortion lobby has claimed that the horror of rape justifies legal abortion. Now, it appears that the profitability of abortion justifies their toleration of rape.

Zach, over the past couple of weeks I have been pleasantly surprised by your willingness to think more deeply about the abortion issue, and to listen to some truths about its supporters. I was pleased to see that you recently "liked" some of my anti-abortion posts on Facebook. The fact that you've been willing to consider arguments on this issue from a conservative Christian—and even to take a public stand that will make you unpopular with your progressive professors and fellow students—gives me hope that you may also be open to discussion of some other aspects of "progressive" thought as well. But before we move on from the subject of abortion, I have one more point I want to make about it in my next letter.

Punishing Abortion

Dear Zach,

Progressives often try to avoid tough issues by labeling conservatives as "insensitive" or "mean." (It's no coincidence that the progressive worldview is behind the current self-esteem movement in public education. It seems much more concerned with producing good feelings than articulating logically defensible positions.) This tendency is often on display when the issue of abortion comes up. You will soon find out that if you decide to speak out against *Roe v. Wade*, you often end up hearing this question: "Do you mean that you would actually seek to incarcerate women who have abortions?"

The question is meant to make you look bad, not to elicit an answer. But you should be prepared with an answer in order to effectively turn the tables on your attacker.

The fact is, even when people see the logic of the argument against abortion, they're still hesitant about the prospect of outlawing it—because they don't want to see desperate women thrown into jail.

So first, you might want to ask the following question, which will expose the question-begging nature of their inquiry: "If abortion kills an innocent human being, should it go unpunished?"

But then you need to provide a detailed answer—that is, if your adversary is willing to listen. My suggested response, in a nutshell, is harsh punishment for abortion doctors and a lesser punishment for women who have abortions. There's a very good legal reason for drawing a distinction between the woman having the abortion and the abortionist performing it, which I will explain below.

Abortion is premeditated murder. In order to convict someone of murder in the first degree, however, the prosecutors must prove more than just premeditation. They must also prove willfulness and deliberation. Finally, they must prove that the defendant's actions were the proximate cause of death.

Proving first-degree murder would be quite easy in the case of the abortionist. Let's examine each element of the

crime separately, as the prosecution must prove each individual element beyond a reasonable doubt:

1. Premeditation means that the killer con-
   sciously reflects upon the desire to kill before
   actually killing. The law measures such reflection in moments, rather than hours or days.
   Given that the doctor carefully prepares his
   instruments and frequently pauses between
   the individual actions that he must engage in
   to perform the abortion, proving premeditation
   should be quite easy.

2. Willfulness means that the killer specifically
   intended death, not just serious bodily harm.
   Obviously, abortion is done for the specific
   purpose of producing death. The doctor
   knows the unborn baby is alive and that at the
   end of the procedure he or she will not be. It
   is his desire to produce death, not injury.
   There is no real ambiguity concerning intent
   in the case of abortion. It would be easy for
   prosecutors to satisfy this element of first-
   degree murder.

3. Deliberation simply means that one has killed
   in "a cool state of blood" in the absence of anything the law considers to be provocation.
   Provocation occurs when the homicide victim
   did something to cause the deadly attack.

A common example is being caught in an act of adultery by a jealous spouse. If one is killed under such circumstances, one is said to have provoked the killing. The killer was not in a cool state of blood and, therefore, did not deliberate. The killing is not excused but instead mitigated to a lesser degree, usually voluntary manslaughter. Obviously, no one can engage in an act of provocation against anyone while still inside the womb. Therefore, it should be easy for prosecutors to establish deliberation on the part of the abortionist.

4. Causation simply involves proving that "but for" the voluntary actions of the accused, the deceased would still be living. This is also very simple in the case of the abortion doctor. A pregnant woman walks in to her appointment at his office. Later the same day, a formerly pregnant woman walks out of his office. Remember that the procedure that ends the pregnancy always stops a beating heart. There is no real question that dismembering the baby is what caused the heart to stop beating and resulted in that baby's death.

Sustaining a first-degree murder charge against a woman who gets an abortion would be more difficult.

She does not perform the procedure so there is, for her, no direct action that results in the death of the baby. In other words, she does not actually commit the offense.

Still, as you will recall from our Trials of the Century course—specifically, from the Manson case—people can be held accountable for acts they themselves do not commit, as long as those acts are a part of a criminal conspiracy.

A criminal conspiracy, however, requires a meeting of the minds.

Zach, the mind of the abortionist and the patient do meet in the sense that they agree on the act of abortion. But they do not fully meet in most cases because the woman rarely knows what the doctor knows—namely, that abortion stops a beating heart and kills a clearly living and obviously human entity. For these reasons, prosecutors would be reticent to charge the patient under a conspiracy theory, and the jury would be unlikely to convict if such a charge came before them. Still, seeking an abortion would clearly be solicitation of a criminal act—a much lesser charge than conspiracy to commit first-degree murder.

If we do overturn *Roe v. Wade*, states would have the right to criminalize abortion and use solicitation statutes to discourage women from seeking abortions in the first place. So I would recommend the following in the case of abortion: 1) a murder prosecution for the doctor, and 2) a criminal solicitation prosecution for the patient.

There is nothing "mean" about punishing abortion. It's exactly the other way around—we are being mean when we see that abortion is murder and then look the other way in order to impress others and enhance our self-esteem.

The Law of Outliers

Zach,

You've been willing to take a public stand on the issue of abortion. Let's move on to a hot-button topic that is getting to be even more likely to cause conservatives to be labeled as "mean" people and "haters"—gay marriage. Gay rights activists want same-sex unions to be legally recognized as marriage, and conservatives want to stick to the traditional definition of that institution. But let's work our way around to that issue from a preliminary consideration of the reason for and importance of laws in general.

A fundamental understanding of laws differentiates adults from children. Any mature system of justice must make tough choices that place the interests of society as a whole above the interests of individuals. An example of such a choice is the decision to differentiate between the legal defenses of "mistake of law" and "mistake of fact."

Imagine for a moment that a student picks up another student's backpack as he is leaving class at the end of a lecture. Before he realizes he has picked up wrong backpack, he is apprehended by the police and charged with petty larceny—that is, taking and carrying away the valuable personal property of another with the intent to permanently deprive the owner of possession.

The student could raise a "mistake of fact" defense. He thought the backpack was his own, so he could not have intended to deprive the true owner of his property.

But imagine that the student tried to raise a "mistake of law" defense. In other words, he admitted he knew that the backpack belonged to another student, but he refused to acknowledge that he knew anything about the crime of larceny. Should the court recognize that as a legitimate legal option?

While courts are willing to accept, with some limitations, the "mistake of fact" defense, they overwhelmingly reject the "mistake of law" defense. The obvious reason for doing so is that such a defense would be subject to widespread fraud and manipulation by guilty defendants. That reason alone provides sufficient justification for the old maxim, "Ignorance of the law is no excuse."

But there is an even better reason to reject the "mistake of law" defense. Put simply, it waters down the moral authority of the law to suggest that it should be contingent upon the subjective perceptions or feelings of the individual perpetrator. The law must be greater than ourselves if it is to hold us in check.

Proponents of gay marriage fail utterly to comprehend the idea that laws are made with society, not the individual, in mind. That is why they also fail to grasp the idea that law is predicated upon averages, not outliers. Interestingly, both libertarians and progressives suffer from this lack of understanding.

The government has an interest in recognizing a traditional marriage between a man and a woman, simply because it has an interest in seeing couples reproduce and then care for their young children. While traditional marriage is good for children, gay marriage is not. Any assertion to the contrary requires willful blindness toward the manner in which gay couples typically live—particularly gay males, who are notoriously promiscuous and unfaithful to one another.

Progressives sometimes directly attack the assertion that the government has a compelling interest in promoting marriage as an institution that is good for children. After all, they want the state to raise everyone's children. Remember "It takes a village"?

But more often they try to undermine the link between marriage and childrearing by pointing to outliers—marriages in which couples choose not to have children or cannot have them because at least one partner happens to be infertile. But this argument only reveals the weakness of the progressive understanding of the law. Put simply, rules that are justified by the average case cannot be undermined by the exceptional case, otherwise known as the outlier. Thus the old maxim, "Hard cases make bad law."

When the United States Supreme Court first took on a challenge to traditional marriage, there was little difficulty resolving the issue. The case, *Reynolds v. U.S.* (1879), involved a Mormon citizen convicted under a federal law prohibiting bigamy. Some familiarity with the origins of the Mormon religion is helpful in understanding the rationale behind the Court's decision.

In the nineteenth century, Joseph Smith claimed to have been led (by the angel Moroni) to a set of tablets he would later transcribe into the Book of Mormon. Smith practiced polygamy—marrying over thirty wives in the course of his lifetime—and he established that practice among men subscribing to the Mormon faith. By the time Reynolds was arrested and convicted of bigamy, the Mormon religion was only a few decades old. In contrast, courts had been recognizing marriage as a union between one man and one woman for many centuries.

Clearly, Reynolds was not a victim of religious discrimination since the restriction of marriage to two persons of the opposite sex *predated* the birth of his religion. His legal arguments failed, and the Mormon practice of polygamy died along with his court case. Being good citizens, the Mormon minority conformed to the will of the majority.

The present political battle over gay marriage is not characterized by a serious discussion of the ramifications of abandoning the traditional definition of marriage. Logically, if we allow for gay marriage we must also allow for polygamous and even incestuous marriages. Remember that the argument used to rebut Reynolds's claim of a right to have multiple wives was that society had long been ordered around a specific and narrow definition of marriage. That argument goes out the window once gay marriage is granted legal recognition.

Imagine for a moment that you are back in the schoolyard as a child in elementary school. It is the first day of a new school year at a new school, and you know none of your classmates. You are named one of two captains in charge of selecting a team to play basketball. If you have any intelligence, you will do your best to pick your tallest classmates, leaving the shorter students to be selected by the opposing captain.

If you can succeed in getting all the taller players, you will win the game. Sure, a couple of the shorter players on the other team could be better than some of your taller players. Those are the outliers, and their existence in no way undermines the rule that taller people are, on average, better at basketball than shorter people.

Your rule of selecting people on the basis of height is an imperfect rule, but it produces the desired result. Only a fool would abandon a winning rule simply because it is not always perfect. Unfortunately, many progressives are also fools.

The government's decision to recognize only unions between a man and a woman has served society very well for a very long time. It may not be a flawless rule, but it has produced the desired results. It civilizes men, it protects women, and it provides a healthy and stable environment for raising children. It performs all of these functions better than any other available option.

Put simply, advocates of gay marriage must understand that our laws are based on averages, not outliers. We lean upon marriage as a cornerstone of our civilization. Some may deem a narrow definition of marriage offensive to their perceptions of fairness and equality. But same-sex unions are not on average equal. Nor are perceptions an adequate basis for law.

Ignorance of the law has long been considered an inadequate legal defense. But ignorance of the basic function of laws is still fashionable in progressive circles.

Liberals N the Hood

Dear Zach,

Last week I wrote to you about gay marriage and our legal system. Today I'd like continue the discussion of legal issues, but focus on crime—and the failures of progressive thought on that subject.

When I first became a professor in 1993, I used to show my students a film called *Boyz N the Hood*. My motivation for showing the movie was that I thought it explained the origins of crime and delinquency in a fair and accurate way. The film fleshes out three different progressive theories of crime and delinquency that have achieved great popularity in academic circles and illustrates how they are supposed to operate in the real world. But now I can see that it also illustrates—though less clearly—a conservative theory of delinquency as well, a theory that is not so popular among criminology professors.

The oldest of the theories, called "strain theory," was popularized in the 1930s. The idea behind this theory is that society imbues all of its citizens with the desire to obtain material things. That much is hard to deny, given our national social emphasis on material wealth and personal success.

The problem, according to the strain theorist, is that society is not structured in such a way as to provide opportunities for everyone to achieve the personal wealth and success that everyone has been inspired to seek. The result of the discrepancy between a) what "society" encourages us to seek and b) what "society" allows us to have is called "social strain."

According to the theory, the more "social strain" we experience, the greater our criminal involvement. So crime should be blamed on a lack of legitimate opportunities for success among the poor. Illustrations of the theory are numerous in the movie *Boyz N the Hood*.

Anyone familiar with the movie recalls the character Ricky, the maternal half-brother of "Doughboy." Ricky is the only one who appears to have access to a legitimate escape route from life in South Central Los Angeles. He is a talented football player and is recruited by top schools such as the University of Southern California. Indeed, the movie makes the point that getting out of the ghetto is difficult and that playing sports is seen as the only path out for many young African Americans. The movie also shows how unrealistic that path is for the average black male.

In contrast, South Central Los Angeles provides a wealth of illegitimate opportunities for success among young African American males. The presence of junkyards in every neighborhood and pawnshops on every street corner cannot easily be ignored. Nor can one ignore their effects on the crime rate. Junkyard owners buy stolen cars without asking questions. Pawnshop owners buy stolen jewelry without asking questions—and there's a great deal of burglary and motor vehicle theft in the hood. And don't forget about the liquor store on the corner. That is where the crime profits are often spent. But the money doesn't stay in the hood because the liquor store's owner usually isn't black.

Another major theory on prominent display in the movie is commonly known as "labeling theory." In recent years, it has become very popular in advancing liberal educational policy. But its origins are in criminology. The basic idea behind the theory is rather simple: if you label a person as "delinquent" or "criminal" then you markedly increase his chances of actually becoming delinquent or criminal.

If you think about your experiences growing up, you may conclude labeling theory has some validity. And if you just think back to the psychology class you had last semester, it may remind you of the concept of the "self-fulfilling prophecy."

When someone gets into trouble with the law once, he is likely to fall under greater scrutiny in the future. That means he is more likely to get caught the next time he does something wrong. Eventually, people stop just labeling the repeat offender's behavior as bad and start to refer to the offender himself as bad—or criminal, or delinquent, or any of a number of negative labels. This eventually damages his self-esteem and creates the conditions necessary for the self-fulfilling prophecy.

The best example of labeling theory in *Boyz N the Hood* is the contrasting ways maternal half-brothers Ricky and Doughboy are raised. The boys have different fathers but are raised by the same mother, who obviously had a better relationship with Ricky's father than she did with Doughboy's father. The mother clearly considers Doughboy doomed to failure because he inherited the genes of a man whom she despises. What she fails to see is that it is her different treatment of the two boys that causes their behavior to move in different directions. The movie tries to illustrate that environmental factor, and it actually does a good job of it.

In the film, Doughboy reacts to the harsh treatment from his mother with rebellion. He is also keenly aware that his mother favors his half-brother Ricky. Whenever something goes wrong, Doughboy is presumed guilty until proven innocent. He is simply never rewarded for doing anything positive. He is also punished for wrongdoing—regardless of whether it was his fault. He has low self-esteem and no incentive to conform, and his life holds little promise.

The final progressive theory of crime advanced in *Boyz N the Hood* is "differential association theory," according to which we are all surrounded by both pro-criminal and pro-conformist influences in our lives. When pro-criminal influences outweigh pro-conformist influences, criminality is the likely result.

Differential association theory recognizes that relationships are an important influence on our lives—especially when it comes to the propensity to commit crime. But our relationships are varied and complex. Differential association theorists talk about four distinct ways those relationships vary in terms of their influence on our criminal tendencies:

1. **Frequency.** Put simply, the more often we spend time with people, the more likely they are to influence our behavior.
2. **Duration.** The longer we know people, the more likely they are to influence our behavior.
3. **Priority.** Relationships established early in life tend to have greater influence on us than those established later in life.

4. **Intensity.** Relationships that have greater emotional intensity tend to carry more weight with people and, therefore, exert a greater influence on their behavior.

Differential association theory in criminology is quite similar to social learning theory in psychology. The social learning theorist would agree that one who is exposed to more pro-delinquent influences than anti-delinquent influences would be more likely to engage in criminal activity. The social learning theorist would also agree that peer pressure is an important part of the social learning process. Clearly, peers you encounter frequently and have known for a long time will have a great influence on your behavior. Also, if you formed the peer relationship early in life, it will influence you greatly—particularly if there is a strong emotional component to the relationship.

All of these factors are on display in the movie *Boyz N the Hood*—particularly in the character Doughboy. He is exposed to heavy doses of pro-criminal influence growing up in the hood. Such influence is only compounded when he goes to prison. When he gets out, he falls back into the old influences that predated his criminal involvement. He is surrounded by very bad people who have been a part of his life for a very long time. And he is very close to those who helped lead him down a path of self-destruction in the first place.

But not all theories of crime are liberal ones that assume people are inherently good until they are corrupted by bad society. "Control theory" is conservative in the sense that it assumes the worst about human nature and asserts that criminal impulses can be controlled by certain positive influences. Control theory is also featured in *Boyz N the Hood*—although less prominently than the progressive theories.

Control theorists believe that explaining crime is not the main task of the criminologist. Since they consider humans to be predisposed toward crime, the focus of control theorists is actually on explaining law-abiding behavior. They ask the following question: How do bad people keep from doing bad things? Control theory offers a four-fold answer:

1. **Attachment.** One way the criminal impulse can be controlled is through guilt. If a young person is attached to a parent—or to a teacher or to some other role model—then he will be less likely to commit crime. The youth knows that the transgression will cause the loved one to disapprove of him, so he conforms. In *Boyz N the Hood*, Tre's attachment to his father keeps him out of a good deal of trouble.
2. **Belief.** In addition to external controls on behavior, there must also be internal moral controls.

Tre's dad spends a lot of time with his son teaching him right from wrong—something few of the other characters in the film experience. Therefore, Tre actually has a positive and pro-social belief system.

3. **Involvement.** This is just a restatement of the old maxim, "Idle hands are the devil's workshop." Put simply, one cannot commit crime while involved in constructive, conformist activities. As soon as Tre's mother drops him off at his father's house (the parents have joint custody), he is assigned various time-consuming chores. While the other kids are off getting into trouble, Tre is raking the yard or otherwise involved in constructive activity.

4. **Commitment.** Tre's father is not the only positive influence in his life. His mother is also a good role model. She is educated and intelligent. She teaches Tre the value of education. Because he does well in school, he is afraid to jeopardize his academic future by getting involved in delinquency.

In the final analysis, *Boyz N the Hood* bears a greater resemblance to the field of criminology than it does to the world of reality. For every conservative explanation of crime, there are at least three liberal explanations of crime.

But in real life it's a different story. The liberal theories of delinquency perform poorly when tested scientifically. In fact, there is probably no other academic discipline that does as poor a job of explaining phenomena over which it claims jurisdiction or expertise as criminology.

When the left-wing theories are actually subjected to empirical analysis, they rarely succeed in explaining over 10 percent of the variation in criminal conduct. To put that in plain English, criminologists often survey people about their involvement in crime. There is a lot of variation in self-reported criminal conduct from one person to the next. Liberal or progressive theorists—proponents of strain, labeling, or differential association—consider themselves successful if they explain 10 percent of that variation in self-reported criminal conduct.

But explaining only 10 percent of the variation in criminal conduct means that 90 percent of the variation remains unexplained. So what do criminologists do with the unexplained variance?

Zach, let's take a step back for just a second. Remember the concept of unexplained variance, from our discussion of studies of racial disparity in the criminal justice system? In the race studies I mentioned before, criminologists assumed that any variance not explained by legal factors could be attributed to racial discrimination—even when racial discrimination was not measured. In other words, unexplained variance equals racism.

If progressives can arbitrarily attribute to racism all of the unexplained variance in sentencing between the races, then what stops us from attributing all the unexplained variance in self-reported criminal behavior to free will? If a progressive theory like labeling is only able to explain 10 percent of the variance in self-reported criminal conduct, then the researcher has only shown that 10 percent of the behavior is determined by the theory. If no other theory is specified, then isn't it fair to say that 90 percent of the variance in self-reported criminal conduct is undetermined? Isn't that just another way of saying that 90 percent of the variance isn't determined by anything? Why not just assume that unexplained variance equals free will?

In the field of criminology, the things criminologists cannot explain are often attributed to racism because that absolves man of personal responsibility. He is seen as a mere victim of his environment. And when criminologists examine man's own self-confessed criminal conduct, the things he (the criminologist) cannot explain are never attributed to free will. To do so would make the man responsible for his own conduct. Such conclusions are simply not allowed in the field of criminology, any more than they are allowed in the world of Hollywood film producers.

In the so-called social sciences, everything is a show. It is always a three-act play directed by progressive thinking. In the first act, man is born innocent. In the second act, man is corrupted by "society." In the third act, the progressive saves him.

The data may show that the progressive worldview is only right 10 percent of the time. But, in his heart, the progressive believes he is right 100 percent of the time. It doesn't really matter what the data say. Progressive thinking isn't very logical. It is often pure emotion feeding on earnest faith in the perfectibility of man. That is the reason why the progressive discipline of criminology hasn't made much progress in the last fifty years.

In January, I'll write to you in more detail about the problems with the leftist understanding of crime. But meanwhile, good luck with your exams, and have a great Christmas break.

How LBJ Abandoned Kitty Genovese

Dear Zach,

Progressive approaches to ameliorating crime—and poverty, which progressives tend to see as the major cause of crime—have not been stunningly successful in the past half century. To understand why, let's rewind to the point in American history, now almost fifty years ago, when those liberal solutions were first being put into practice.

The spring of 1964 was a difficult time. The Warren Commission was trying to heal the wounds caused by the Kennedy assassination and to bring closure to a murder case that would never reach trial. Lyndon Baines Johnson was trying to step out of the Kennedy shadow and forge a new direction for the American people. Then, one March night in New York City, a killer stepped out of the shadows and opened a new set of wounds—not just on his intended target, but on the conscience of a nation.

Kitty Genovese was attacked shortly after 3:00 a.m. outside her apartment in Queens, New York. Her attacker was a man named Winston Moseley. When he initially attacked her, she started screaming. Her screams were said to have been heard by thirty-eight people—none of whom did much to help her. Some lights came on in the apartment complex where Kitty lived. Someone shouted something at Moseley, and he went away for about ten minutes.

But Winston Moseley came back and resumed his attack on Kitty Genovese. She had been injured too badly to get all the way back inside her apartment. So she was extremely vulnerable when the attack resumed. Moseley did not meet much resistance when he started stabbing her again. He punctured both her lungs and then raped her as she lay dying. An ambulance arrived, but it was too late. She died around 4:15 a.m.

There have been some challenges to the notion that thirty-eight people heard the screams of Kitty Genovese without coming to her aid—a number as low as twelve has been suggested. But regardless of the exact number, the incident inspired a line of research by social psychologists into what is now referred to as the "bystander effect." This

behavioral effect is said to stem from a psychological process known as "diffusion of responsibility."

The idea behind the bystander effect is that we should
not assume that it is unusual for a victim to go unassisted
despite the presence of numerous witnesses or passersby.
The victim may go unaided *because of* the presence of
numerous witnesses or passersby. This makes sense for a
couple of reasons.

A bystander could be reluctant to help someone when
others are around because of a feeling that the others might
be more qualified to help. For example, if some injured
person is lying by the side of the road after a nasty fall,
someone who lacks medical expertise may decline to help,
assuming that there is a nurse or even a doctor among the
other bystanders.

But also the presence of others may give a bystander
an "out" in a situation where he simply does not want to
help. By saying to himself, "Someone else will probably
help" (diffusion of responsibility), he can justify walking
away and leaving the task to someone else (bystander
effect).

The *New York Times* ran a story on the Kitty Genovese
case two weeks after the attack. The author of the piece
pulled no punches in describing a city—and a society—that
had become calloused and indifferent toward those in need.
Were there no Good Samaritans among the thirty-eight
who were eyewitnesses to (or who at least heard) the attack

on Miss Genovese? The attack seemed to speak volumes about the coarseness of American society.

The attack on Kitty Genovese came at a turning point in the history of our nation's approach to controlling crime. Just a few months earlier, President Johnson had taken the reigns of government under tragic circumstances. Just a few weeks earlier, he had given his first State of the Union address. In that address he had promised to push through civil rights legislation that had failed during Kennedy's abbreviated term as president. He had also promised an unconditional war on poverty.

President Johnson's message was twofold: 1) Poverty is caused by societal factors including, but not limited to, racial discrimination, and 2) it is the responsibility of the government to solve problems like racism and poverty.

The non-response to Kitty Genovese's cries for help is in some ways a symbol of a deep transition in American life. It had always been assumed that the answer to the question "Am I my brother's keeper?" was a resounding "Yes." But the unspoken theme of President Johnson's Great Society was, "The government is my brother's keeper."

Of course the causes for the change that seemed to be crystallized by the Genovese case are more profound and complicated than just Johnson's policies. A president's agenda can affect a society in profound ways, but big changes take years, not months. The encroachment of the social welfare state in America would not have been possible without a significant decline in Christian charity. In fact, it would not even have been necessary.

Camelot

Zach,

One of President Eisenhower's most enduring contributions is the interstate highway system—something few twenty-first-century Americans can imagine life without. Ike was first inspired to undertake this initiative shortly after the invasion of Normandy on D-Day in 1944. After troops had landed, they had some difficulty navigating the back roads of France. Those navigational difficulties impaired the American troops' ability to drive the Nazis back into Germany and finish the war. When the Americans finally did make it to Germany, they found that the

Germans had a much more sophisticated roadway system than the French. Ike never forgot that, and as president, he was determined that in the U.S. the road system would be modeled after the one in Germany.

But sometimes broad government initiatives can have unanticipated consequences. Eisenhower's interstate highway initiative is no exception to the rule. While it made interstate travel easier, it also changed the nature of our neighborhoods and affected the nature and prevalence of interpersonal crime.

The United States began construction on the interstate highway system in 1956. During the next decade, America saw the greatest crime increases in its history. Serious crime increased by more than 100 percent in the span of a decade. Without question, the principal reason for that drastic increase was the baby boom. Because we had an unprecedented number of babies born in the mid-1940s, we had an unprecedented number of teenagers in the 1960s. Because people are most likely to commit crimes while in their teens and early twenties, the 1960s saw a serious crime wave.

But anyone alive during the 1960s can tell you it was a complicated and turbulent decade. Many factors helped drive up the crime rate. It doesn't take much imagination to figure out how changes in our transportation system contributed to crime increases. We have long known that serious crime is higher during the summer months, simply because people are out and about and therefore exposed to one another with greater frequency. To the extent that people are out in public, they become targets of interpersonal crime. And while they are away from home, they are also more likely to be victims of certain property crimes such as burglary.

The interstate highway system contributed to this problem by making our country smaller. It has given those who are motivated to commit violent crimes easier access to potential victims and has allowed them to escape more quickly to destinations that are farther away.

Transportation has also changed the nature of crime in America. Before we had an interstate system, the most violent crimes were between people who knew one another. Over the last several decades, interpersonal crimes against total strangers have been on the rise. The Internet has accelerated this trend—creating, in effect, a new virtual interstate highway system that brings people closer together, for both good and bad purposes.

In this interconnected nation of ours, people travel not only for illicit reasons but also for legitimate business reasons. The nationwide business chain has replaced the small-town store. The changing nature of business means that people are likely to change jobs often, which increasingly means working in new and unfamiliar cities. Since people move so often, it is not surprising that fewer of us get to know our neighbors.

Last summer, I had a long discussion about all of these changes with an old friend of mine named Jeff Chambers.

I had not seen Jeff in years, as we had lost track of each other for nearly a decade. He had moved so often that it was tough for us to keep in touch the way we once did. When we began to reminisce about the old days of our childhood, he used a word that I found interesting. He referred to our old neighborhood as "Camelot."

I remember the first day our families met. It was during the summer of 1969 (please, no references to stupid Bryan Adams songs!). My mother used to go down to the water authority to get the names of families who had just moved to the area and had recently opened new water accounts. That's how she found out that the Chambers family had moved into the apartment complex right across the street. My mother took me over to their house so we could introduce ourselves and invite them to church.

After they joined our church, my family started to spend time with theirs once a week when our parents played bridge together. I spent every other Saturday at the Chambers family's apartment playing G.I. Joes with Jeff and his younger brother Chris. They spent every other weekend at ours. To top it all off, my dad and Mr. Chambers joined the church softball team. Our families were inseparable.

Our families were not the only ones that were close. We had a huge network of other families that kept in touch even after we moved out of those apartments and into our first little houses. Looking back on it all reminds me of an important principle of what's called "routine activities theory" (related to "control theory," which I wrote about in connection to *Boyz N the Hood*)—the idea that the nature and prevalence of crime often has less to do with the decisions of criminals than it does with the routine everyday activities of non-criminals.

When people are out of their homes working and traveling extensively in a vibrant economy, they are more likely to be subjected to the risk of interpersonal crime. When people do not take the time to get to know their neighbors, they are less likely to have someone watching over their homes. They are even, as in the case of Kitty Genovese, less likely to have someone willing to personally watch over them.

In the neighborhood Jeff Chambers remembers as "Camelot," people got to know their neighbors personally and learned their habits and proclivities. They were able to detect when something was wrong and then felt an obligation to intervene. That feeling is more likely to occur when the person next door is your *neighbor*—not just the person next door.

The progressive worldview, as we have seen, assumes that human beings are naturally innocent, and that crime has to be explained by something outside them—poverty, or the influence of society. Thus the "social strain," "labeling," and "differential association" theories of crime are developed. The "routine activities theory" is more compatible with the Christian and conservative worldview which takes a realistic view of human nature—namely, that the world is full of people who are motivated to commit crimes. But motivated offenders are unable to commit crimes unless they come into contact with suitable targets (like Kitty Genovese) in the absence of capable guardians (such as concerned neighbors).

The central idea of routine activities theory, the equation that "crime = motivated offender + suitable target – capable guardian," has obvious application to the realm of violent crime. But its application to property crime is even more compelling. That will be the subject of my next letter.

The Case for Transistor Control Legislation

Zach,

I know you don't like your present off-campus job very much, but I want you to imagine a job far more risky and far less rewarding. I want you to imagine that you are a professional burglar in the early 1950s. I mean that literally. I want you to stop what you are doing and imagine trying to commit the crime of burglary in an average neighborhood in an average town during the decade after our soldiers returned from World War II.

Progressives argue for gun control on the theory that when guns are readily available, crime increases. In fact, there's a lot of evidence that just the opposite is true. I'll write in some detail about gun control in a future letter. But in this letter, I'm going to make a similar case for transistor control legislation.

Prosperity was on the rise in the 1950s, but people still did not have much in the way of electronic gadgets. Whether we are talking about electronic inventions that make life easier or about devices used for entertainment, there simply was not much to be found in the average home—at least compared to today. And the electronics that did exist were built with cumbersome vacuum tubes, not silicon transistors.

If you looked into a living room window and tried to "case" a house for a burglary, these are the kinds of things you might have found: a television set weighing well over one hundred pounds; a radio (on top of the TV) with huge "rabbit ears" antennae protruding from its top; and perhaps a stereo system with turntable, receiver, and speakers all welded into one highly immobile audio entertainment system.

What you were also likely to see was a housewife doing chores, or worse—from the perspective of the burglar—staring right at the TV that you would like to steal if you had the opportunity. And that is really the key word in the present narrative: "opportunity."

"Routine activities theory,"—which, like the "control theory" that I explained in the context of *Boyz N the Hood*, is compatible with man's fallen nature—posits that crime equals a motivated offender plus a suitable target minus a capable guardian. If that's the case, then you as a burglar in the '50s are in very serious trouble. Since these valuables inside the living room are very heavy (not suitable targets for stealing) and a housewife seems to be virtually always home (and capable of guarding them), you would seem to be out of luck. If you want to burglarize this home, you had better wait until the whole family is on an extended vacation. And you had better bring some friends and a U-Haul to help cart off the stolen merchandise.

Now take a few minutes to imagine what it would be like to be a burglar today. Imagine yourself planning the burglary of an average house in an average neighborhood in an average town. If you peered into the living room window, here is what you might find: a television set weighing about twenty pounds, a DVD player weighing no more than five pounds, and a stereo system with CD player, receiver, and speakers—each component separate and weighing less than five pounds. You might also see a laptop weighing just a few pounds and an iPod weighing just a few ounces.

Remembering that crime really equals a motivated offender plus a suitable target minus a capable guardian, you are in very good shape. Because these valuables inside the living room are very light (suitable targets for stealing), and the husband and wife seem to virtually always to be at work (and thus incapable of guarding them), you would seem to be in luck. If you want to burglarize this home, you do not have to wait until the whole family is on vacation. And you will not need to bring friends and a U-Haul to help cart off the stolen merchandise. Just bring an empty laundry bag and a Honda Civic. You'll be able to clean the place out in a few minutes.

This illustration seems to paint a dismal view of crime in the twenty-first century. It is true that modern technology has created an abundance of suitable targets for property crime. But there are ways to increase capable guardianship in order to offset the effects of modern technology—ways that stop short of banning the transistors that make electronic devices lighter and easier to steal.

Back in the 1990s, Marcus Felson wrote a book called *Crime and Everyday Life*, which offers cause for optimism in a society vulnerable to predatory crime. In that brilliant book, Felson explores ways of increasing capable guardianship without spending a lot of money.

For example, he discusses the desirability of building a short picket fence around your home, instead of a tall brick wall. It may seem counterintuitive, but the latter invites burglary while the former does not.

To illustrate Felson's point, imagine yourself casing a house surrounded by an enormous brick wall. It might be tempting to pass on the opportunity because the wall is high and somewhat hard to scale. But once you are over the wall you have it made. Passersby cannot see what you are doing once you get inside the yard. The large wall operates as a shield to allow you to take your time as you break the lock and eventually rummage through potentially valuable papers and personal effects hidden in the house.

But a short picket fence has the opposite effect. Once a burglar is over the fence everything that he does is in plain view of passersby. He had better pick the lock quickly and close the blinds as soon as he gets inside. Otherwise, a jogger or dog walker just might call the police on a cell phone and spoil his fun.

Another of Felson's examples of how homes and businesses can be designed in such a way as to increase capable guardianship is the decision of a convenience store chain to make some experimental changes in accordance with the central idea of routine activities theory, that crime equals motivated offender plus suitable target minus capable guardian.

The convenience store chain had long had a routine habit of posting advertisements in its windows, which were all located in the front of the store. It also had had a habit of installing its cash registers in the back of the store. Putting the registers in the back had seemed to make intuitive sense—the robber would have a longer distance to travel on his way from the register and out the front door as he tried to flee the scene of the crime.

But the convenience store chain decided to experiment with a new plan that was initially twofold: 1) They removed all of the advertisements from the front windows of the store, and 2) they placed the cash register right behind the windows in the very front of the store.

Later, the convenience store would add two more innovations: 1) They placed the cash register and clerk on platforms, so that customers had to look upwards toward them—and potential robbers could not see how much money was in the cash register at any given time—and 2) they painted the word "taxi" on the parking space directly in front of the front doors of the convenience store. In addition to allowing taxis to wait there free of charge, they also offered cab drivers free coffee and restroom privileges.

With these simple innovations, the store slightly reduced motivated offenders' access to suitable targets.

But the innovations also *more* than slightly increased the presence of capable guardians. There the change was dramatic. For example, people who passed by before the innovations were made could not see a robbery taking place in the back of the store, especially with the windows covered by advertisements. But looking through clear windows at a robbery taking place in the front of the store—with the panicking victim elevated above all else—was simply impossible to miss. And best of all, the first person likely to witness the event would likely be a cab driver whose car was equipped with a CB radio.

I don't have to tell you the results of the experiment. You already know that the incidence of robbery dropped dramatically. (Otherwise, why would I be telling you this long story on an afternoon when Duke is playing North Carolina in the ACC conference final?)

This approach to combating robbery is very clever. It does not require expensive progressive social engineering in the form of building schools or raising the minimum wage. The grossly naïve principle that doing good things for people will lead them to return the favor by doing good things for "society" is nowhere in the equation.

Instead, this approach to fighting robbery assumes the worst about people—they will commit crimes if they have the opportunity. Then it proceeds to block opportunities for crime by increasing visibility, making crime that much more difficult to commit—and it does so for little more than the cost of giving cheap coffee to taxi drivers.

But of course, increasing visibility is only effective in preventing crime if people feel some obligation to help one another—to be capable guardians. That is why we must continue to teach people to love their neighbors and do for them the things they would wish done for themselves.

After fifty years of trying to implement new and clever progressive theories of crime prevention, it has become clear that the same features that made the neighborhood I grew up in a kind of Camelot are still the most relevant factors. When it comes to fighting crime, community is a far more important word than government.

I'm looking forward to more correspondence and discussion with you after spring break, Zach. Until then, go Heels!

Government Subsidies and Spousal Abuse

Dear Zach,

I was sorry to hear about your bad experience with your cell phone service provider over spring break. At the risk of giving you unsolicited advice, let me say that it probably wasn't a good idea to sell them your cell phone based on their promise that your upgrade would be available for pick-up in the store the next day. You were naturally shocked when you went to the store and they told you it was not there and would not be there *for another month.* But I wasn't shocked when you told me. Your service provider is subsidized by the federal government, and that makes a difference in the way they treat their customers. Because you did not know that, you are without a cell phone for the next month.

I wasn't shocked because I had a similar experience with the same federally-subsidized cell phone provider that just dealt with you so dishonestly. They were once in charge of providing my cell phone and Internet services. When I found out they were charging me 50 percent more than a local competitor, I called to cancel my Internet service. Distraught over the prospective cancellation, they matched the other company's offer, and I stayed on with them. But then they did the same thing to me that they did to you—they broke a promise upon which I had relied.

Zach, I recount the following events not just because they are educational, but because they are also downright comical:

Customer Service Visit #1: I went down to customer service to cancel my Internet service because the cell phone service provider had continued to charge me under the old rate for two months, despite their promise to make the rate change effective immediately. They apologized and said it would not happen again.

Customer Service Visit #2: Ten months later, they raised the rate again, specifically to its previous level. So I went down to tell a customer service agent to cancel my service. They said they did not want to lose me, and they restored the lower rate.

Customer Service Visit #3: One year later, they did it again. So I went down to talk to a customer service agent and asked what the problem was. They told me the low rate was just a temporary promotional offer, which had expired. I told them to cancel my service. They said they did not want to lose me and offered to restore the lower rate. I took them back. That was stupid of me.

Customer Service Visit #4: For two consecutive months, they kept charging me the higher rate. So I went back to cancel my service. It was a Saturday and the young woman working there apologized and told me that she would work everything out on Monday. I left hoping that my relationship with my provider would be improved by her intervention.

Customer Service Visit #5: I got a call from the aforementioned customer service representative, telling me that she could not restore my rate until I came back in the store to talk with another

representative, who would then fix things immediately. I came in to the store only to hear a face-
less representative tell me over the phone that
we could not work things out. That is, she could
not offer the lower rate. When I told her to cancel
my service, the girl tried to negotiate a new deal.
That's when I just lost my temper and let loose
with something like the following:

"You know, you're not really an Internet provider.
You're nothing like one. You're more like an abu-
sive spouse. You treat me disrespectfully until I
threaten to leave you and then you promise to
make things better. But they only get better for
a while because you don't change. You just lie to
me to get me back because you can't live without
me. But this time I mean it. We're through!"

There were two employees in the store when I unleashed
that little salvo. One was simply speechless. But the other
was actually laughing because she knew that I was right. I
really do enjoy using humor—especially when I feel like I
am about to have a stroke. But Zach, there is a serious point
to be made here. The question is, what the heck does it have
to do with the political problems we've been discussing?
Well, everything. Please allow me to explain.

When the government gets involved in trying to solve a problem, it invariably makes things worse. Your cell phone provider—my previous Internet provider—is subsidized by the federal government. For that one reason, and that one reason alone, you are unlikely to ever get good service from them. Because the federal government has built a safety net beneath it, it is not afraid of falling. That is why its employees behave so carelessly towards you. Doesn't that make sense, Zach? It's basic human psychology.

Furthermore, when the federal government gets involved in something, it's even worse than when the local government gets involved. The reason for that is simple—the greater the physical distance between the problem and problem-solving entity, the less likely you are to find an effective solution. Local problems can't be efficiently solved by national agencies.

So far in college you have been exposed to a lot of theory. But I want you to get a healthier dose of reality. So I have a little assignment for you—two assignments, actually:

1. Take a notebook with you the next time you go off campus to get your driver's license and vehicle license plates renewed. Those renewals are handled by two separate agencies. One is run by the government. One is privately operated. Take notes and tell me which agency was more

efficient in their dealings with you. Then I will
tell you which one was privately operated.

2. Take that same notebook with you every time
    you go to the admissions office, parking office,
    or financial aid office here at UNCW. Two of
    those offices are controlled by the state govern-
    ment. One office is controlled by the federal
    government. Record enough information about
    your experiences to report back to me with a
    reasonably detailed evaluation of each experi-
    ence. Then I will tell you which one is run by the
    federal government.

Thinking about these issues will actually help you nav-
igate the current political climate. Our politicians are
increasingly asking us to trust the government with ever-
greater involvement in our affairs. However badly government messes things up, the solution is always more
government.

Zach, in my opinion, these politicians sound a lot like
your federally subsidized cell phone provider. They keep
saying that things will get better if you just give them one
more chance. But deep in your heart you know they're
lying—and they'll just make you look stupid all over again.

We Don't Need No School of Education

Zach,

Just last semester I terribly offended an education student who was enrolled in my introduction to criminal justice class. I know I offended her with my split infinitives. But I also offended her by suggesting that we ban the Watson School of Education from the UNC-Wilmington campus. What can I say? I like to boldly go where no other infinitive-splitting professor is willing to go.

From time to time, I joke around about things we need to eliminate on our campuses. But I was not kidding about the Watson School of Education. I believe it should be banned. My reasons are twofold:

1. Education majors do not earn a degree in any substantive discipline. They merely learn to "educate." The obvious question: Educate about what? Why not have them earn a degree in a substantive area like history or English and then learn how to "educate" people by serving a longer term as a teaching assistant? Currently, they only do a one-semester teaching assistantship. Whatever happened to the idea of longer-term apprenticeships? It seems like we hear more about apprenticeships on reality TV shows than we actually see of them in reality.

2. Education majors are indoctrinated heavily in postmodern philosophy, which teaches them that there is really no such thing as objective truth. No one doubting the existence of objective truth should be trusted with the responsibility of teaching anyone at any level.

In our desperate attempt to elevate the self-esteem of students, we have succumbed to the postmodern temptation to eschew objective truth. In the process, we also eschew the notion of objective falsity.

I am not the only one who has noticed this phenomenon. Rita Kramer authored a classic book called *Ed School Follies,* which dealt with the issue at great length. In her well-researched book, she documented how one education professor taught future teachers how to acknowledge wrong answers. The list of possible responses: "Um-hmm," "That's a thought," "That's one possibility," "That's one idea," "That's another way to look at it," and "I hear you."

Notably missing from the list: "That's wrong." I suppose the professor would have thought it wrong to conclude that an answer could possibly be wrong. But there really is something seriously wrong with never telling students they are wrong.

Sometimes I think we are moving in this direction in order to boost the self-esteem of teachers. No one wants to be the "meanie" who goes around correcting small children. But these people are learning how to to be teachers. That's their job.

I Earned My B.S. in Victimology

Zach,

Sometimes I have a hard time convincing people that the things I write about in higher education are actually real. I even have a hard time convincing them that some of our courses and majors truly exist. One good example is a course called "victimology," which is frequently taught in our department. I have little doubt that before long Victimhood Studies will become an actual major housed in its own freestanding academic department.

As I look forward to the prospect of a victimology department turning out victimology majors, one question immediately comes to mind: what else could victimology majors do with their degrees except become professional victims?

It should be noted that there are numerous degrees already in existence that prepare students to become experts in certain types of victimhood, so a victimology major would be redundant to some extent. No doubt you have heard of some of these majors already being offered at a number of American universities:

1. **Women's Studies.** This is a major that teaches women to consider marriage a form of patriarchal oppression and motherhood a form of slavery. Women are taught that they are so victimized by men that the word "women" should be changed to "womyn" to avoid any association with men.

2. **Gay, Lesbian, Bisexual, Transgender, and Queer Studies.** Some of the same lessons learned in Women's Studies are retooled in these programs using slightly different terminology. For example, marriage is seen as "heterosexist" rather than patriarchal. Both mean the same thing: oppressive.

3. **African American Studies.** Black people are seen as the victims of white people, and affirmative action and endless reparations for

slavery are the necessary remedies for this
oppression.

4. **Hispanic Studies.** Same idea, different race.
The public policy initiatives advanced in these
programs include open border immigration
policy, bilingual education, and out-of-state
tuition waivers for Hispanics who are victims
of their parents' decision to enter the country
illegally.

One wonders why victimology is even needed as a
course of study within the field of criminology. All of these
other degrees are essentially specialized varieties of Victimhood Studies. They are taught by people who see themselves as victims and are bent on showing other people how
they are victims, too. The only real career these degrees
prepare one for is teaching some variety of Victimhood
Studies. The whole field of victim education is both self-
perpetuating and entirely useless for anything but lifetime
employment within itself.

Of course, in a sense, people who major in any variety
of Victimhood Studies really do become victims upon
graduation. That is when their student loan payments are
due, and either they have no job or their salary is too small
to make the payments. At that point, there is nothing left
to do but take to the streets and blame their capitalist
oppressors.

I have a novel idea for these protestors: Why not pack up, leave Wall Street, and move the protest to the local university? That's where the people who taught them that victimhood pays are. Professors pushing different versions of victimhood are the true reason these kids have buried themselves in a mountain of debt and cannot escape it. They should demand a refund from the local university and leave the capitalists alone. It isn't the capitalists' job to clean up the mess created by those who could never survive in the private sector.

The Fear of Ideas

Dear Zach,

One morning in January of 1993, as I was walking down the hall in the sociology building at Mississippi State University, I saw my good friend (and professor) Greg Dunaway. When he saw me he shouted a question, "Hey, Mike, weren't you a Sigma Chi?" I replied "Yep. I still am." He continued, "I think one of your guys got murdered last night. A guy named Steckler and his girlfriend, too."

I thanked him for letting me know, rushed out the door, and drove across campus to the fraternity house. By the time I got there, a couple of reporters had arrived. The mood in the house was somber. It would stay that way for weeks.

The facts of the case are sad and gruesome. Jon Steckler and Tiffany Miller left the fraternity house around one in the morning. As they crossed the parking lot and approached Jon's car, they saw a man trying to break into another car parked nearby. Tiffany shouted at the man to stop what he was doing. And he did.

But when the thief turned around, he was brandishing a gun. He immediately ordered Jon and Tiffany to get into Jon's car. The man hopped in the back seat and ordered them to drive to the outskirts of town. Before they knew it, Jon and Tiffany were taking their last ride together in his car. They must have known those were the last few minutes of their lives. The only question was what that man would do to them now that he had assumed full control of their destiny.

About ten miles outside of town on U.S. Highway 45, the man ordered Jon to pull over. There on the side of the road he murdered both of them execution-style. Later testimony revealed that Jon was forced to watch his girlfriend take a bullet in the head shortly before he suffered the same fate. To add fatal insult to fatal injury, the armed sociopath would later try to blame the killings on rap music.

At the time of the murders, I was a liberal who was opposed to handguns. I had even voted for Michael Dukakis in 1988 in part because of his support for a complete national ban on handgun ownership. But I was also playing in a band and had to travel late at night—sometimes driving more than sixty miles home after the bars shut down at midnight.

Every Thursday night I played at a bar called Jefferson Place in Tupelo, Mississippi. On the way home, I had to pass by the very spot on Highway 45 where Jon and Tiffany had been murdered. I usually passed by the murder site between one and two in the morning. I started having nightmares about the killings. And I started to think about guns in a different way.

A good friend of mine by the name of David Lee Odom, who also owned one of the bars I used to play in, invited me to go shooting with him just a few weeks after the murders. David had just purchased a .44 magnum and was looking to sell a .357 magnum. So we went out to the local gun club one Saturday afternoon and fired off a couple hundred rounds.

After just one day at the shooting range, I agreed to buy his gun—a Smith and Wesson Model 19 revolver—for $250. I tucked it under my seat every time I took a road trip in my old Toyota truck. I knew that if the truck ever broke down I would not have to worry about being caught unarmed by an armed criminal, the way that Jon and Tiffany had been. The playing field would be leveled by my two new friends, Mr. Smith and Mr. Wesson.

Although I bought that first handgun in 1993, I did not get around to applying for a permit to carry a concealed weapon (CCW) until 1997. By that time, I had moved to North Carolina to teach criminology at UNC-Wilmington. My decision to acquire the concealed carry permit was prompted by a drug trafficking problem in the neighborhood where I bought my first house. There were crack dealers living just a few doors away, and I wanted to be armed on those occasions when I would walk from my house to downtown Wilmington—especially when I had to go to the ATM and walk back to my house with a wallet full of cash.

Upon hearing that I had obtained a CCW, one of my colleagues—a criminology professor—made an interesting comment. He said that the research indicating that CCWs actually reduce violent crime was "unsettling" to him. The remark is certainly an odd one for a criminologist to make. Why would anyone, particularly anyone who had devoted his professional life to acquiring expertise on crime prevention, be bothered by the results of research suggesting that a public policy was actually achieving its goal of reducing crime?

The answer, of course, is that reducing crime is not the chief concern of many criminology professors—or of professors in general in the so-called social sciences, even though crime is one of our most serious social problems. They are often more interested in having their own preconceived notions confirmed. Such bias does not advance knowledge. If fact, it only impedes it. It is one reason why our universities have become ideological echo chambers.

Of course, nothing other than a wildly naïve worldview could explain the profound bias against guns so often expressed by liberal academicians. They don't like guns for the simple reason that guns—like prisons and military bases—are reminders of human imperfection. If one simply relinquishes one's naivety concerning human nature, it is easy to see how easing gun restrictions can reduce crime. In fact, the logic behind CCW laws meshes perfectly with our previous discussions of routine activities theory.

The motivated robber is always looking for a suitable target. So he is always aware of the nonverbal cues communicated by potentially vulnerable targets. (If such cues were impossible to detect, or unimportant, our U.S. Air Marshals would not spend so much time training agents to identify potential hijackers by examining nonverbal signals.)

The individual who is carrying some sort of weapon also carries *himself* differently from someone who is unarmed. The average citizen is not as nervous when he is carrying a weapon—even if he is walking alone somewhere in the dead of night. He is, therefore, very unlikely to nervously avert his gaze from passersby. The motivated offender knows such a person is not a suitable target for a robbery.

I know this is true from personal experience. I have rarely been approached by panhandlers since I obtained a CCW permit. Of course, many people are uncomfortable carrying handguns. And that is fine because they also benefit from CCW laws. The reason is simple—capable guardianship.

In jurisdictions where concealed carry permits are easy to get, if someone should decide to rob the unarmed citizen, there is a good chance that a law-abiding witness to the robbery will be carrying a concealed weapon. Instead of being a mere witness, the armed citizen is a guardian capable of thwarting the robbery. Everyone benefits—except, of course, the motivated offender.

Since every law-abiding person benefits from CCWs, it is difficult to understand the opposition to them. Believe me; the opposition is often emphatic and emotionally charged. That was crystal clear during our last faculty meeting in the Sociology and Criminal Justice Department here at UNCW.

We were talking about emergency evacuation plans and what we should do in the event that a shooter decided to come into the building and embark on a shooting rampage. The conversation went on for about twenty minutes before someone asked what they should do if someone came into the classroom and found them (the professor and the students) while they were hiding underneath their desks. The answer—coming from someone who actually has a Ph.D.—was an instant classic: "Throw a book bag at him!"

I didn't know whether to laugh or to cry. If either Jon or Tiffany had a book bag on them that night, might they still be alive today? I don't usually speak up at department meetings, but this time I asserted the obvious: "No school shooting in American history has ever targeted a criminal justice department."

I also gave the rather obvious reason: "This absence of shootings in criminal justice departments is explained by the fact that many criminal justice students are armed law enforcement officers finishing their degrees between shifts."

Of course, any potential shooter knows that police officers major in criminal justice—and student police officers carry their service weapons to class. I summed up my brief statement with the following plea to end the pointless discussion:

"Since we—unlike other departments—have student police officers coming to class with guns, no shooter is going to target our building. We can talk about a shooting in this building all day long, but it just isn't going to happen. There's no need to practice throwing our book bags. Our armed law enforcement officers will protect us."

This should have been comforting to my fellow professors, but it wasn't. One of the women sitting across the room from me just buried her head in her hands and shook her head back and forth in disgust. The rest of the room fell silent. I could have told them I supported the legalization of incest and gotten a warmer reception. After the meeting, one of the professors walked up to me and said, "I hate guns. We just have a difference of opinion, Mike." My response was measured:

"In reality, there is no difference of opinion between us. There have now been sixteen refereed academic studies demonstrating that CCW laws reduce violent crime. There has been none showing that these laws increase violent crime. When we allow CCW permit holders to carry their guns on campus, all the other buildings will be just as safe as ours."

She was polite and listened to what I had to say. But after I finished she just looked at me and said, "I guess I'm not familiar with the research." Then she walked away. But the truth of the matter is that my colleague will never familiarize herself with the research in this area—despite the fact that she teaches criminology. Instead, she will just continue to hold an opinion based on her professed hatred of guns. But it would be more accurate to say that her refusal to change her opinion is based more on the fear of ideas than the hatred of guns.

In January 2007, three months before the Virginia Tech shooting that killed nearly three dozen people, there was a proposal before the Virginia legislature to extend CCW laws to allow permit holders to carry their weapons on public college campuses. The proposed legislation did not pass.

Imagine how things might have been different if college professors in Virginia had been "familiar with the research" on CCW laws. Imagine how things might have been different if college professors in Virginia had been willing to lobby the legislature to ensure the passage of a bill that, according to the research, could have been expected to reduce crime.

Imagine a world in which professors cared more about combating violence than reinforcing their pre-existing biases and broad assumptions in favor of the inherent goodness of man. Imagine no more ideologues. It's easy if you try.

Tolerance Presupposes a Moral Judgment

Zach,

Last week, I was standing at the podium getting ready to give a lecture when I noticed that a young woman had her laptop computer out. You know I don't allow laptops in the classroom, so I was especially amused when I noticed that the outside of her computer was adorned with a bumper sticker that said "TOLERANCE" in big white letters. Ignoring her plea, I demanded that she put her computer away during the lecture. I simply don't "tolerate" students who pretend to take notes on their laptops while they are, in fact, surfing the web and posting on Facebook.

But I do seriously wonder whether she—or any other student promoting tolerance—really understands what the words means. It is unlikely that she does, given the fact that most of her professors do not understand what it means either. Even professors sometimes mindlessly repeat words they don't understand. "Tolerance" and "diversity" are arguably among the most often repeated and least understood words in higher education today.

To illustrate my point, I am forwarding an email I received from a colleague announcing the showing of a pro-homosexual film at the Lesbian, Gay, Bisexual, Transgender, Questioning, Inter-sexed, and Allied Center at UNC-Wilmington:

Gentle folks~

I know that I'm "taking a chance" forwarding this to you all. I know that some are <u>intolerant, unaccepting</u> and "not comfortable" with "the gay lifestyle." But someone has to have some *huevos* around here and that would be me.

Jimmy Wheeler had hopes and dreams. He was a gifted poet and painter and had a loving family who supported and cared for him. But for Jimmy Wheeler, growing up gay in rural Pennsylvania was too much to take. He was abused regularly at school. He was called awful names. In 1997, alone in a cold room, Jimmy Wheeler took his own life. "Jim in Bold *tells the story of young James Wheeler and tells the stories of gay youth in this country, from the tragic impact of hatred to the triumphant resilience of youth" said Equality Forum's Executive Director Malcolm Lazin.*

The first and most amusing thing you probably noticed about this email is that its author congratulates himself on the courage he exhibited in sending it. His bravery in this instance is debatable since I am the only conservative Republican on the list of professors to whom it was sent. The other two dozen professors in my department are either independents or registered Democrats. Several are Marxists, and almost all of them are staunch supporters of the "gay rights" movement. So sending this email to the department is about as courageous as sending a racist email to a bunch of Klansmen.

This professor's email was the third I had received promoting this "coming out" film. When I received the first notice (from the LGBTQIA Center), I simply deleted it without comment. When I received the second notice (from my department chairman), I again deleted it without comment. Next, my colleague sent the alert out a third time with a judgmental statement that not only applauded his personal courage but characterized those who disagree with him as "intolerant" and "unaccepting." At that point, I decided to write about it.

Obviously, the professor who wrote this email is not willing to tolerate intolerance. Nor is he willing to accept un-acceptance.

The point that my colleague lacks tolerance— at least for those of us who subscribe to the Judeo-Christian world-view—is too obvious. In fact, he is so intolerant and unac-cepting of those he considers intolerant and unaccepting that he must underline the words "intolerant" and "unaccept-ing."

What is less obvious is that he also lacks tolerance toward homosexuals.

In order to tolerate something you must first disapprove of it. Since my colleague approves of homosexual conduct, he cannot simultaneously tolerate it. Let me illustrate with a couple of examples.

- I approved of the recent killing of Osama bin Laden by U.S. Navy Seals. Therefore, it is not possible for me to "tolerate" their actions as an unfortunate necessity of war.
- I approved of the decision of Springfield Armory to send me a free personally engraved .45 semi-automatic handgun. Therefore, it was not possible for me to "tolerate" their benevo-lence.

The problem with professors like my colleague is two-fold: 1) they often use words that they do not understand and 2) they often claim to be morally superior to others on the grounds that they do not believe they are morally superior to others.

The profound illogic of diversity moralists like this professor can be annoying at times. But as the lone conservative Christian in the department, it's just something I've learned to tolerate. After all, maybe they didn't choose to be sanctimonious hypocrites. Maybe they were born that way.

Fox and Foes

Zach,

Speaking of things progressives won't tolerate, I want to discuss Fox News. Let me tell you about a conversation I once had with a parent I ran into in the cigar shop. He was riled up about an assignment his freshman daughter had been given on the topic of global warming. The assignment was for credit in an environmental science class.

For the assignment, she was allowed to use cable news sources and Internet sources. The only restriction was that she could not use Fox News as a source. The parent was angry because he is a conservative and likes to watch Fox

News. I agree with the parent on this issue. In fact, I see two problems with this assignment.

First, there is the problem of using cable news and Internet sources for college research assignments. I would generally not allow either one to count as a legitimate research source for a student seeking college credit. I want students to use books and journal articles as references.

Second, there is the issue of banning Fox News—and only Fox News—as a source for the paper. This move was predicated on the notion that Fox, despite its claims to be "fair and balanced," really is a biased, unfair, and imbalanced news source. This belief, which most professors seem to hold, is so confusing that it will take a little time to untangle. Please, be patient.

If one is interested in seeing a biased, unfair, and imbalanced news source, then one need not get cable or satellite television. One need only turn on the regular evening news. It does not matter whether one is talking about ABC, CBS, or NBC, nor does it matter what topic one is talking about. Let's use the topic of abortion as an example.

Whenever a major news network like CBS runs a segment on a women's issue, such as abortion, they interview an expert. (Note: They see abortion as a women's issue. I see it as a human rights issue). The expert, however, is always a representative from the National Organization for Women (NOW) or a similarly pro-choice group. It is never a representative from a conservative group like

Concerned Women for America or Phyllis Schlafly's Eagle
Forum.

Of course, because the selected expert always takes the
liberal position—the pro-abortion position, in this case—
there is no fair opportunity for the other side to present its
view. Nor is there a balanced presentation of the issue, since
only one side is presented. This is an example of biased
reporting since the network is liberal and the one side they
present is also liberal.

In other words, CBS is unfair, imbalanced, and biased.
That's why I rarely watch them any more.

My experience with Fox News has been much different.
I was first involved in a nationally publicized free speech
controversy in 2001. That controversy revolved around an
accusation of libel that a socialist student leveled against
me. After she tried to demand that the university read some
of my private emails, I was invited to appear on Fox's
Hannity and Colmes. They invited my accuser, too, but she
declined to appear on the show.

Then, in 2003, I wrote a controversial satire on affirmative action. I was invited to appear on *The O'Reilly Factor*
to discuss my position. Bill invited someone on the other
side of the issue to appear on the show as well. That person
declined, and I made my appearance on the show without
opposition.

In 2005, I got into a bit of a tiff with an anti-Semitic,
Holocaust-denying professor. We were invited to appear

together on *Fox News Live* with Martha MacCallum. I showed up, but the anti-Semite did not.

In 2007, I linked a Kent State University history professor to a violent Islamic Jihadist website. I specifically accused him of treason for aiding and actively encouraging the killing of American troops (and for disseminating bomb-making instructions on the Internet). We were both invited to appear on *Fox News Live* with Megyn Kelly. I showed up, but the professor did not.

You are no doubt seeing a pattern here. Fox News may be biased, but the apparent imbalance is often created by leftists who refuse to debate the issues on Fox. In fact, one Marxist actually mocked Fox publicly about their claim to be "fair and balanced"—after declining to debate me on Fox News. To me, that sounds like killing both your parents and then asking the judge to show you mercy because you're an orphan.

As for the decision to ban Fox as a resource for that environment science class assignment because of its "bias," only this needs to be said: the professor sees the speck that is in his brother's eye yet is blind to the log in his own.

But what is to be said about the rest of the Fox News-haters, Zach? Is it accurate to say that professors with leftist politics hate Fox News *despite* its desire to promote debate on controversial issues? Or is it more accurate to say that these professors hate Fox News *because of* its desire to promote debate on controversial issues?

Regardless of how you answer that question, I hope we can agree on one thing: most people who teach at secular universities have no business lecturing others on the issue of ideological diversity.

Rester in Peace

Zach,

My seventh-great-grandfather was a man named Frederick Rester. I learned about him through my mother's tireless efforts to trace our family history as far back as possible. She managed to trace those roots back to the 1500s. She even traveled to a small Lutheran church our ancestors attended in Germany in the wake of the Protestant Reformation.

In the nearly forty years during which my mother researched our family, there was nothing that interested me more than Frederick Rester's story. The reason for that was simple: he was a veteran of the American Revolution fighting under the leadership of General George Washington.

Frederick Rester went to battle for this young nation at the age of thirteen. He was shot and received an honorable discharge from the military at the age of fifteen. I have a copy of his official discharge. It is among my most cherished possessions.

But until a couple of years ago, when I began to read biographies of all our American presidents, I did not gain a full appreciation for the sacrifice of our revolutionary soldiers. I started with George Washington, of course, and was shocked to learn of the conditions our troops faced during the American Revolution.

Reading about soldiers who crossed the Delaware River mid-winter without any shoes made me wonder whether Frederick Rester was among those barefooted soldiers. It also made me think about the pathetic condition of today's men—a generation so indifferent to principle and so intolerant of discomfort. I began to notice the contrast when I left school and became a college professor.

When I accepted a job as a university professor back in 1993, I was so excited because I have always considered the American university to be the quintessential marketplace of ideas. I looked forward to contributing to that robust marketplace by addressing many of the great controversies and issues of the day. You can probably imagine my disappointment when I first discovered that our university employed a patently unconstitutional speech code.

It was just my first semester, the fall of 1993, when I sat down and read our university speech code, which was embedded within our university's faculty handbook. The code said there was a ban on the use of offensive speech—anything which might make someone feel uncomfortable along the lines of race, gender, and a whole laundry list of other demographic variables.

As I sat in the department's main office and read our speech code, I was so taken aback that I had to read it again out loud. After I read it out loud, I looked up and said, "Every idea is potentially offensive to someone. Every idea has the potential to make someone feel uncomfortable. This speech code is clearly unconstitutional."

A colleague who happened to be present responded, "But the speech code doesn't apply to all kinds of speech. It only applies to certain types of speech." No truer words were ever spoken.

After I heard my colleague's frank admission, I knew that some day I was going to have to go to war against that speech code and against university speech codes in general. I was a liberal and an atheist at the time, but I knew I had a legacy to defend. I could not simply hand over the rights Frederick Rester fought so hard to defend. Apathy did not seem rational at the time. And I'm still surprised that this idea of a ban on offensive speech has been adopted by so many otherwise rational people.

From our discussions of abortion and criminology, you've already seen that leftists have trouble with arguments, research, and facts that don't conform to their view of the world. Speech codes are one way for them to force people with dissenting views to shut up. Personal attacks are another. If you're going to be challenging the progressives' assumptions in public, you're going to have to be ready to deal with those attacks.

I will write more on that in my next letter to you, which will also take up some of the differences between liberals and conservatives on economic issues. Meanwhile, study hard and enjoy this beautiful spring weather.

The F-Bomb

Zach,

There is a growing divide in America between two groups—those who believe the government can solve all of their problems and those who desperately want to see the government get out of their way so they may live freely and solve their own problems through their own abilities. Unfortunately, those in the former group have a tendency to attack their political opponents with words they do not even understand. America's continuing financial problems have really brought this tendency to the forefront of American political discourse.

Last summer, Standard & Poor's decided to downgrade America's credit rating from AAA to AA, marking the first time America had lost its AAA rating since the Great Depression. Within days, liberal advocates of deficit spending began to refer to this downgrade as the "Tea Party downgrade." In other words, progressives began to say that the downgrade that resulted from deficit spending was actually the fault of a political movement that opposes deficit spending. This is a lot like saying that feminists can be blamed for the problem of rape or that the NAACP is responsible for the problem of lynching.

To make matters worse, Congresswoman Debbie Wasserman Schultz, a Democrat from Florida, had already referred to the Tea Party as a bunch of "tyrants." That is certainly odd because the Tea Party is comprised of individuals who would like to end government tyranny by drastically reducing the size of government. The illogic of her remarks reminds me of a comment characterizing me as a "fascist" for supporting Tea Party favorite Michele Bachmann in the race for the Republican Presidential nomination.

That was the third time I had been called a fascist by someone characterizing himself or herself as a progressive. See if you can identify the common thread among the three accusations:

1. In 2000, a colleague hurled the accusation against me after he saw an NRA sticker on my office door.

2. In 2004, another professor hurled the accusa-
    tion against me—she actually used the term
    "fascist pig"—because I missed a party at her
    house in order to attend a "Friends of the NRA"
    dinner. In fact, she was so angry that she said we
    were all "fascist pigs."

3. Finally, in 2011 I was dubbed a fascist by some-
    one who thought I was a part of the Tea Party
    movement. Actually, I am not—although I do
    respect what they are trying to do.

The common thread here is pretty obvious. The accusation of fascism is a response to my support of limited government and increased private ownership—most notably,
my support of the private ownership of firearms. This would
seem to be at odds with the true definition of "fascism,"
which follows (from the *Merriam-Webster Dictionary*):

> A political philosophy, movement, or regime (as
> that of the Fascisti) that exalts nation and often
> race above the individual and that stands for a
> centralized autocratic government headed by a
> dictatorial leader, severe economic and social
> regimentation, and forcible suppression of oppo-
> sition.

That's odd, isn't it? Those who favor collectivism above
individualism and who approve of centralized government—

characterized by *increased* economic regimentation—are using the term "fascist" to describe the opponents of their positions—which progressives, in fact, share with actual fascists. This is not to suggest that all progressives are just modern-day fascists. But it does suggest two other things that are worth noting in **bold letters**. (Sorry, Zach, I don't like to use ALL CAPS in emails but I do occasionally use **bold letters**.)

1. **Many members of the progressive movement do not seem to understand the meaning of the word "fascist."**
2. **Fascists probably have much more in common with progressives than they do with members of the NRA or the Tea Party.**

But, of course, progressives have trouble understanding the truth of the second **bolded** statement because of the undeniable truth of the first statement. That is why I wish some of these progressives had met my fifth grade teacher, Mrs. Barbara O'Gara.

When I was just eleven years old, I got into an argument with a classmate. For the life of me, I cannot remember what we were arguing about at the time. But I do know that I was losing the argument because I also lost my temper. And then I blurted out the accusation that my classmate was a "fascist." Mrs. O'Gara stopped what she was doing and immediately focused the attention of the class on yours truly. The first question she asked was simply devastating: "Mike, what exactly is fascism—in other words, what does one have to believe to be a fascist?"

I was utterly terrified. Because I did not know the meaning of the word "fascism" or the word "fascist," I simply sat there and shook my head. I was then given a homework assignment: go home and look up the meaning of the word "fascism" and return with a brief one-paragraph, typewritten explanation of the word—followed by a brief one-paragraph explanation of why it is generally a bad idea to use words you don't understand.

There is a lesson to be learned from this. When we are involved in heated arguments we do not usually have the authority to assign homework to our opponents. But we do have the opportunity to ask them these two questions, loosely based on Mrs. O'Gara's strategy for dealing with me:

1. What exactly does "fascist" (or any other derogatory term) mean?
2. What does "fascism" (or any other derogatory term) have to do with the situation at hand?

When we ask these questions, it is very unlikely that we will get a response to the first question. In other words, we will usually end up supplying the definition of the derogatory term to the person who interjected it into the conversation in the first place. Whenever we ask the second question, we have an opportunity to completely turn the tables on our opponents.

Of Mice and Mensa

Dear Zach,

Before we go any further, I want to remind you of the reason why I began writing you this series of letters. When I first taught you as a freshman at UNC-Wilmington, I had very high hopes for you and for your future intellectual development. But the second time I taught you—in the spring of your sophomore year—I noticed that you had embraced some of the ideological assumptions and beliefs of some of your progressive professors. Because I think that their ideology is both wrong and dangerous, I wanted to continue the conversation. You've shown yourself to be remarkably willing to consider another point of view, to face facts and logical arguments that didn't mesh with the beliefs you had adopted, and to rethink some of the positions that you had taken. Now I want you to think about why you adopted those progressive positions in the first place.

It is beyond dispute that many students like yourself move to the left during their college years. What is disputed is the reason why they do so. Generally speaking, there are two competing common explanations for this phenomenon:

1. **The Discrimination Thesis.** This view says that students are liberalized in college because they are exposed disproportionately to liberal and progressive ideas. In other words, they are brainwashed.

2. **The Enlightenment Thesis.** This view says that students are liberalized in college because they are simply becoming more informed, educated, and enlightened. In other words, they are simply converging on the truth, which is the progressive point of view.

The *Seahawk*, our student newspaper, once did a story about liberalism on campus, specifically probing the question of whether there was a "liberal bias" in higher education.

The story quoted a UNC-Wilmington professor who took the position that there was no such bias. He argued that 1) better educated people tend to be more liberal (because they are more educated) and that 2) people who are more educated get hired to teach (because they are more educated, not because they are more liberal).

This argument suffers from the following fatal flaws:

1. **The observation that he pointed to in support of the enlightenment thesis is equally consistent with the discrimination thesis.** Both sides in the argument acknowledge that people tend to become more liberal as they become more educated. The question is why. The discrimination thesis, no less than the enlightenment thesis, accepts the correlation between years of education and acceptance of liberalism. But it ascribes that correlation to a lack of exposure to conservative ideas, and a lack of criticism of liberal ones.

2. **The enlightenment thesis is at odds with current educational philosophy.** To believe that people are simply enlightened by further education is to assume that there is some sort of objective truth upon which people can converge. This is totally at odds with the educational philosophy of the postmodern liberal university. The

postmodernists who hold sway in university education would ordinarily bristle at the notion that there exists some sort of truth that is not either a) culturally determined or b) determined by some sort of power elite defending its own interests.

3. **Aside from these logical flaws, the enlighten- ment thesis is countered by objective data suggesting that anti-conservative discrimina- tion is widespread.** For example, several years ago a sociology professor in my department constructed a survey designed to determine whether there is, in fact, widespread political discrimination at UNCW. The sociologist was, of course, a liberal, and the survey was seriously flawed. One of the questions on the survey, which was given to UNC-Wilmington employ- ees, asked whether the respondent had ever been denied a job at UNC-Wilmington. Of course, it does not take a membership in Mensa Interna- tional to figure out that it's especially unlikely you'll find people denied a job at UNCW among a population that is *employed by UNCW*. But the survey was only given to people who worked at—read: were, in fact, hired by—UNCW. (There goes the argument that liberals have a monopoly on the world's intellectual firepower.)

But, despite the severe flaws in the survey instrument, this study nevertheless discovered systematic evidence of discrimination against conservatives. I know this because the evidence was referenced in a UNCW press statement. Shortly after I filed suit against UNCW for denying me promotion to a full professorship, a reporter wanted to interview someone from the university in order to get their reaction to the suit. University officials declined the interview. Instead they issued a statement rejecting my contention that the denial of promotion was due to political reasons.

In that press statement, the university claimed to be "surprised" by survey results showing that people had experienced political discrimination at UNCW. The survey they were referring to was, of course, the one conducted by the liberal sociologist in my department.

When the study was later published, in 2010, its own liberal author reported finding that all groups surveyed were more likely to report "a bias against conservatives than against Liberal and Moderates." Notice that she displayed her own bias by capitalizing "Liberals and Moderates" and putting "conservatives" in lower-case letters. She also reported that "Conservatives were more likely to report a need to conceal their beliefs." (That time, she capitalized "Conservatives," but only because it was at the beginning of the sentence.)

Zach, does "liberal bias" seem like a fair way to describe the situation in higher education today?

Profiles in Anonymity

Dear Zach,

It was great to get a chance to talk to you again during my office hours on Friday. It's good to know that your junior year is ending on a high note. I really enjoyed our discussion about personal courage, and the willingness to stand up for the things you believe in, in a hostile environment. That's the topic I'll be writing on today. Even if all you're fighting for is widespread acceptance of ending sentences with prepositions, I want you to advance it with unapologetic courage. That's what many of our brave soldiers died for. I mean the freedom to advocate your cause, not the sentence-ending prepositions.

As you can imagine, it makes me wince every time I see a college professor—especially one with the full protection of tenure—shirking his responsibility to speak the truth and to do so with conviction. Unfortunately, most professors only have convictions before they enter the teaching profession—and most of those convictions are drug-related. I'm only kidding, but sometimes I have to make jokes like that just to keep myself from crying.

Recently I was reminded of the appalling state of spinelessness among contemporary college professors. It happened when I found a series of three anonymous notes posted above my mailbox in the Department of Sociology and Criminology. Each one of them was in response to a column I had written publicly and to which I had attached my name. Each note is worth describing, along with the circumstances that provoked it.

The first note simply asserted that the Tea Party was not a legitimate grassroots movement because it was propped up by Rupert Murdoch. The note was left above my box shortly after I defended the Tea Party publicly. My defense of the Tea Party also questioned those who classify the movement as "extreme" and "racist." The note did not really offend me because I'm not actually a member of the Tea Party. So I just ignored it.

The second note specifically said, "God is a theory and evolution is a fact." It was pinned above my mailbox shortly after I wrote a column criticizing the theory of evolution. Charles Darwin actually referred to evolution as "my [Darwin's, not Adams's] theory." So, I printed off a quote from Darwin, highlighted the phrase "my theory," and pinned it next to the note above my mailbox. But I added my name to my note because I am generally opposed to leaving anonymous notes. It is only acceptable to leave anonymous notes in grammar school. By middle school, the practice should be avoided. I feel the same way about bedwetting and talking to imaginary friends. At some point, one has to evolve beyond these practices.

The third note said, "God is the world's greatest abortionist. 25 percent of pregnancies end in miscarriage within two weeks. That's intelligent design in practice!" Unsurprisingly, this note was provoked by a column I wrote on the topic of abortion. There was little sense in responding to this note since its contradiction was self-evident. In sentence one ("God is the world's greatest abortionist."), the author accuses God of killing babies on purpose. That's what an abortion is—an intentional termination of pregnancy. In sentence three ("That's intelligent design in practice!"), the author accuses God of killing babies by accident, apparently because God is not intelligent enough to design miscarriage-proof babies. The further insinuation is that if God cannot create babies with a success rate above 75 percent, then He cannot possibly have created the universe.

Of course, even a mentally handicapped child knows the difference between harming someone unintentionally and harming someone on purpose. Who could possibly fail to grasp the parallel difference between abortion and miscarriage? One is an intentional act, the other isn't.

Frustrated by the stupidity of the notes and by their anonymity, I spoke to the professor who occupies the office across the hall from my mailbox. I just asked him who had been leaving the notes. I first suspected it was a graduate student, but I was wrong. According to the professor, who can see my mailbox directly from his office, it was a fellow professor who was leaving the notes. That professor should have grown out of the practice of leaving anonymous notes, but at this point that is unlikely to happen. He is over fifty years old.

The case of the professor who leaves anonymous notes for his colleagues is symptomatic of everything that is wrong with Godless progressivism. This professor has had tenure for years. His tenure protects him from ever losing his job for saying something controversial. But he doesn't believe in God, and without God, there can never be real security. That is why so many progressives are so lacking in courage once they step outside of the classroom and away from a captive audience of teenagers.

I share this with you because this is where progressivism can lead students who don't grow out of it quickly. Unless you choose a radically different path, one day you'll lack the ability stand up for the truth because you will have convinced yourself that it doesn't really exist. I want you to lead a better life—one in which you may be ridiculed for standing up for things you believe to be true. It is the only life worth living. It beats the alternative of anonymously defending your unbelief.

Zach, your willingness to hear challenges to your progressive beliefs over the past year has been extraordinary. It's an unusual student who is willing to reconsider, based on facts and logic, once he has adopted the angry attitudes of his liberal professors. But I hope you can be an even more extraordinary person. I want you to become a lightning rod for the truth—a man constantly pushing buttons and constantly causing people to come after you. I don't want you to end up an old man sneaking down a hallway and leaving anonymous notes for people you are afraid to confront—just because they hold ideas you cannot rebut.

I won't be writing again for a couple of weeks, during the usual end-of-semester time crunch. But after I finish my grading I'll be heading back out to Colorado, and when I get there, I'll write you again—this time on the subject of the experience I had that caused me to abandon progressive politics altogether.

Meanwhile, I hope your exams go well!

PART TWO

THE HEART OF THE MATTER

*"Political problems, at bottom, are
moral and religious problems."*
—Russell Kirk

The Constitution Is Dead (Because God Isn't)

Dear Zach,

It's hard to believe we've been corresponding for more than a year now. Once again, the weather here in Colorado does not bode well for the global-warming apologist. It is 48 degrees in the middle of the day in the middle of May—exactly one year after I wrote my first letter to you from this same spot. The light mist has just turned into a light rain.

During the course of the past year, we have discussed some problems with the progressive worldview. You've seen some logical errors in progressive thinking—and also some signs that a leftist worldview can have strange effects on the people who adopt it.

Now I want to get to the heart of the matter. Progressive politics—in fact, the whole progressive worldview—is really built on one huge mistake.

As I write, the clouds are descending upon Pikes Peak and making their way toward my little cabin at the base of the mountain. It is so much like that afternoon in March of 1996—March 7 to be exact—when I walked inside the gates of a prison in the Andes Mountains just outside of Quito, Ecuador. The weather was the same that day, but everything else in my life was different then.

I was an atheist trying to save the world. I was also a criminologist and an aspiring journalist hoping to change what was going on inside those prison walls. I did not know that what was going on inside those walls would forever change me. The existence of God, the fallen nature of man, and the source of our inalienable rights would all come into focus in a few short hours.

That prison was the closest thing to hell I have ever seen.

First I made a brief visit to the inside of a thirty-six-square-meter cell packed with forty-five inmates. There was the unbelievable stench of rotting meat being thrown into vats of boiling water to make it barely edible for the inmates. There were puddles of urine mixed with fecal matter sitting near broken and rotting pipes. There was the young man I saw being badly beaten by baton-wielding guards. I still remember the sound that club made as it struck against his bones. He was probably no more than eighteen years old.

At the end of the prison visit, I met a man who was awaiting trial for petty larceny. Even though punishment for the offense was usually only a couple of months, he had already been in prison for two years awaiting his trial. I spoke to him about his plight. He told me he missed his wife and his little girl. But there was a peace about him that still haunts me to this day.

Inside that man's bunk were a Bible and a picture of Jesus. The man's eyes filled with tears as he thanked me for coming to talk to him that day. "No one knows we are here," he insisted. "No one cares that we exist," he added as he smiled and shook my hand.

There are political consequences to religious principles. As a matter of fact, political differences tend to boil down to religious differences, when you get to the heart of the matter. There is a statue of the Virgin Mary that sits atop a hill overlooking that small prison. It was the first thing I saw after the guard shut the prison gate behind me. I stood there in the light drizzling rain and stared up at that statue. "I was wrong," were the only words that came to me. I was looking upward as I spoke them audibly.

What I meant to say was that I had been wrong about atheism and the path I had been following for years—a path toward a worldview based on moral relativism. That path had led me nowhere. No honest person can witness the things I saw and hear about the things I heard about in that prison and flippantly dismiss right and wrong as cultural conventions.

The clubbing of the boy was simply wrong. Serving rotten meat to prisoners is simply wrong. Shocking confessions out of prisoners by wiring their genitals to car batteries is simply wrong. Telling prisoners they are free to go, shooting them in the back as they are walking out of the prison gates, and then reporting the incident as a thwarted escape attempt is simply wrong.

And of course it does not matter where or when such things take place. They are wrong everywhere you go. They will still be wrong long after you and I are dead. The moral law is not contingent upon our feelings or our perceptions. It stands outside of us and is eternal.

Think about the following question for a moment: If you suddenly decide the law of gravity is relative—that it's not a universal absolute—will you go floating off into space? Of course you won't. It is the same with the moral law. You cannot escape it. It is written on your heart, but it is not bound by the thoughts or feelings of any man.

That afternoon in Ecuador, I came to understand that the source of that moral law written on everyone's heart is God. That's why I believe that God is seen most clearly when we cast our eyes upon abject evil. C.S. Lewis said that the shadow proves the sunshine. The shadow simply cannot exist without the light.

That day at the prison is also the point at which my progressive political beliefs began to unravel.

As I said earlier, there are political consequences to religious principles. Again, as a matter of fact, political differences tend to boil down to religious differences, when you get to the heart of the matter. There is a reason, for example, why the atheist is more likely than the theist to see our constitution as a living, breathing document. Because he does not believe in God, he cannot believe in an absolute moral law or in God-given rights. He thinks rights are given by man. But if that's true, man can also take them away.

Beware of the man who believes our constitution is living and breathing. In all likelihood, he believes that God is dead. As Dostoyevsky taught us, if there is no God, then anything is permissible—including torturing prisoners to get confessions, suppressing free speech, and cruel and unusual punishments—all the things that our "dead" constitution prohibits.

What I began to understand in that Ecuadorean prison so many years ago is that everything good, right, and true in this world depends on God. Wherever the reality of his existence and his standards are rejected—well, let's just say that the results are really ugly.

What I am asking you to do at this point is to take a definite stand on the side of the good, right, and true and against the ugliness that's so apparent in some of the politics on our campus. I hope that by this point in our correspondence you're convinced that facts and logic are on the conservative side of the argument. But now I am asking you to take a leap beyond facts and logic—into faith.

In my next two letters, I'm going to tell you the stories of two men who did just that.

Like a Good Neighbor

Zach,

Jimmy Duke was a NASA engineer who sometimes attended our church in the early 1970s. By the mid-1970s, he had left his job as an engineer to start his own insurance agency with State Farm. As the result of a tragedy, he had also left the church, and he wouldn't return for about thirty years.

The tragedy did not affect his family but instead that of a good friend. It all happened quite suddenly. His friend's young daughter was thrown from a car and killed instantly when she was struck by another car moving along the highway. Jimmy could not understand the death of his friend's young daughter. He simply could not square it with the idea of a loving God. So he left the church. That's how a lot of people leave the church, I'm afraid.

At first Jimmy Duke didn't really stop believing in God. He just questioned God's moral authority to take the life of an innocent child. But once you declare God to be an unjust God you begin to move toward atheism. No one wants to believe in a God that isn't just. So eventually they just stop believing.

In 1976, Jimmy Duke became my pitching coach on a team called the Red Sox, which eventually won the Little League Championship (with me playing first base). As a die-hard Yankees fan, I can hardly believe that I once wore a Red Sox hat. But I'm glad I did. It gave me a chance to become better friends with the coach's son, Jim Duke, who was also a pitcher. We had actually known each other since we were in the same second grade class in 1972. But playing together on a winning team made us much better friends.

In 1977, my family moved into Jim Duke's neighborhood. We lived just one street away from my former teammate and former coach. So we became even better friends in our junior high and high school days. Long after I went off to college at Mississippi State, and even after Jim went to its SEC rival, Auburn, we remained close friends. Jim was a groomsman in my wedding in 2003.

Good, solid, long-term friendships are of immense value—especially when tragedy strikes, as it did in 2005. Jimmy's ex-wife, Sandy Duke, was diagnosed with cancer and died during the late summer of the year. The last few weeks of the sickness were brutal. She was in constant pain and in need of constant supervision. Thank God that Jim and Jimmy were both living and working nearby, and thus able to be there in her last days on earth.

Sandy and Jimmy had divorced in the late 1980s, but they had a strong friendship in the years that followed. Their relationship was so good that Jimmy and his second wife Linda were both regular visitors at the hospital during Sandy's last days. The way they treated one another after their divorce was a good example for their children, Jim and Gwendolyn. But it was more than that. It was also a good example for all who knew them.

Jimmy was devastated when Sandy passed away. The senseless death of a child had driven him from the church thirty years before. So he had no church to help him process Sandy's slow and painful death. There was a void in his life and he knew it. Senseless human suffering may have driven him away from God. But, now, senseless human suffering was drawing him back.

He was certainly confused. So one day he walked into Barnes & Noble and began perusing the apologetics books in the religion section. There were so many of them that he left the store in frustration on several occasions. After a few weeks and more than a few visits, he settled on a book called *I Don't Have Enough Faith to be an Atheist* by Norman Geisler and Frank Turek.

Jimmy read the book from cover to cover. Then he read it again. And then he read it a third time. Somewhere in between, he read the Acts of the Apostles from the New Testament. When he was done with his reading, he made a full and complete return to Christianity.

Then Jimmy Duke called a meeting of all his employees at State Farm. There were several dozen of them. Jimmy's business had grown a lot since the 1970s when it was just Jimmy and a secretary in a cramped office next door to a 7-Eleven convenience store. As the employees sat and listened attentively, Jimmy told them he had just had a religious conversion, and he wanted to let them all know how it was going to affect them as employees.

Jimmy started out by telling all the employees that they could go to the Holy Land any time they wanted, if it was something they desired to do. He said that he would give them time off from work and that he would pay for their trip. Then he went on to say that he would pay their tuition if they wanted to take courses in religion at one of the local colleges or universities. Finally, going even further than that, he offered to pay for their divinity degrees if any of them felt called to serve the Lord in ministry. Then he simply dismissed the meeting and walked out of the room.

Everyone in the office must have been stunned by the sudden turn of events. But it would not be the last time they would be stunned by a sudden turn of events in Jimmy Duke's life. Just a few months after his conversion, Jimmy was diagnosed with a rare blood disease. By the summer of 2006, he was lying on his deathbed. It was only about a year after Sandy had passed away.

That was a tough period for my friend Jim. Within the span of that next year, he had to watch both of his parents die. Fortunately, Jimmy's death was a little faster and less excruciating than Sandy's. In fact, the ending of Jimmy's life really was a happy one, and I mean that literally. As Jimmy Duke lay dying, his son asked him how he was doing. He was too weak to speak, so he reached for a pen and a piece of paper. He wrote only one word in response to Jim's question. That word was "HAPPY."

To the best of my knowledge, that was the last word Jimmy Duke ever expressed on this planet. For thirty years, he was angry at God. But in the end he was happy. He died happy, and there is only one explanation for that happy ending.

But I'm not done with the story yet. I decided to write a review of *I Don't Have Enough Faith to be an Atheist*, the book that helped lead Jimmy Duke out of his unbelief and toward a very happy ending.

Actually, I had intended to review *I Don't Have Enough Faith to be an Atheist* for quite some time. Rush Limbaugh's younger brother David had recommended it to me back in 2004. When I heard about Jimmy's conversion, I decided to make the review of the book an unusual one. I would simply tell his conversion story and let it speak for itself.

The day I ran my column on TownHall.com, I got a "thank you" call from Frank Turek, who lives just four hours away from me in Charlotte. Later that day, I got another special call. It was Frank's co-author, Norm Geisler. Norm was calling to tell me that the column moved him so much that he was brought to tears before he finished reading it. Talking to him was a great honor and a great source of joy. We would finally meet in person in the summer of 2010, largely as a result of the column—but I'm getting ahead of myself now.

There was a reason why Norm's call meant so much to me. I used to read his books when I had realized I was lost and was making my way back to Christianity. It was almost too much to digest—how people like Jimmy Duke continue to influence lives even after they are gone. But Jimmy's influence on my life was just beginning.

Over the course of the next two years, I became very good friends with Frank Turek. In the spring of 2008, Frank would be the first person to tell me about a great place in Colorado called Summit Ministries. Early that summer, Frank called Summit President David Noebel to tell him he should invite me to speak at one of their student worldview conferences. In July, I flew to Colorado to speak at Summit. The experience changed my life.

In 2008, I spoke at just one Summit student conference. In 2009, I spoke at three. In 2010, I moved out to Colorado for the entire summer in order to speak at seven consecutive student conferences. That first full summer in Colorado was great. While I was there, I met Norm Geisler. I also met a lot of great college students who were serving as Summit staff members.

One staffer I will never forget was named Kristen Kay. We started talking one day when she saw me wearing my Yankees hat. She told me her grandfather used to play for the Yankees in the '50s and '60s. Then she told me one of the greatest redemption stories I have ever heard. It was a lot like the story of Jimmy Duke. But it involves someone you have definitely heard of before. The story is a long one and the hour is getting late. I'll try to write again tomorrow.

Mickey's Last at Bat

Dear Zach,

I want to tell you about an hour-long interview that I was able to do with Yankee great Bobby Richardson last Christmas break. He's the grandfather of Kristen Kay, the Summit staff member I told you about in my last letter. Kristen was kind enough to arrange an interview with Mr. Richardson, who was gracious enough to accept. I've wanted to talk to him ever since I learned about his relationship with Mickey Mantle, the great Yankee Hall of Famer. I was lucky enough to meet Mickey Mantle when I was just a young boy. He's the main reason I'm a Yankees fan today.

Shortly after I met Kristen Kay and told her I was a Yankees fan, I got a very special package in the mail. It was from Bobby Richardson. Inside, there was an autographed picture of him holding the bat he used to set the World Series record of 12 RBIs back in 1960. There was also a pamphlet inside that told the story of Mickey Mantle's conversion to Christianity in the final days of his life. That story teaches a valuable lesson I want to share with you.

Mickey was raised in a home with an alcoholic father and a Christian mother. His mother took him to church throughout his childhood and adolescence. The lessons he learned in the church stayed with him in his later years. They eventually helped facilitate his own acceptance of Christ shortly before his death.

Like many young men who fall away from God, Mickey's decline had been a slow one—even though his rise to fame was fast. The Yankees drafted him when he was only seventeen years old. Within five years, he won baseball's coveted Triple Crown by hitting the most home runs and the most RBIs and batting for the highest average in the American League. Before he retired, he won the American League's Most Valuable Player award three times. He was also probably the fastest player in the major leagues.

Mickey quickly became a legend and was admitted to the Hall of Fame during his first year of eligibility. His fast living was also legendary. Unfortunately, it would continue long after his retirement and induction into Cooperstown.

Bobby Richardson and Mickey Mantle played their last major league game together on October 2, 1966. That was the year Bobby retired from baseball. Although he was four years younger, he retired three years before Mickey. In retirement, they saw each other several times a year, on average, for over three decades due to the numerous Old Timers' games they played together, beginning when they were both relatively young men. Bobby told me he made his debut as an "old timer" when he was just thirty-three years of age.

According to Bobby, nearly every time they were together during those retirement years, Mickey told him that he knew he needed to come back to the Lord. But he kept putting it off. That was mostly because of the shame and regret he carried with him. He had wasted most of his life on booze and hard living. He had been a bad husband and a bad father, and he knew it. Finally it all caught up with him in the summer of 1995.

Bobby had one last chance to sit down with Mickey that summer, just a few days before he died. When he paid his last visit to Mickey in Baylor Hospital, the legendary Yankee pitcher Whitey Ford was just walking out of the room. That would be Whitey's last visit with Mickey.

Bobby walked into the hospital room, went over to the bed, and saw that Mickey had a smile on his face. The first thing he said was, "Bobby, I've been wanting to tell you something. I want you to know that I've received Christ as my savior."

In a very simple way, Bobby said, "Mickey, I just want to make sure." Then he went over God's plan of salvation with him—that God loves us and has a purpose and a plan for all of us; that he sent his son, the Lord Jesus Christ, to shed his blood; and promised in his word that if we repent of our sins and receive the Lord Jesus that we might have everlasting life. Mickey said, "That's what I've done." Just a few days later, Bobby Richardson repeated that story at the funeral of Mickey Mantle. I'm repeating it to you today for a reason.

Mickey drifted away from the truth and from the sense of right and wrong that his mother had worked so hard to instill in him. He barely recovered and was able to secure his salvation with just a few short days left in his life. Nonetheless, his story is being used for a greater good. Every time it is told, it helps bring meaning to a life that seemed to have been squandered chasing after things of little value. I tell it to you today for much the same reason I told you the story of Jimmy Duke.

Jimmy Duke was more fortunate than Mickey in the sense that he had some time to share his story with others. In that wonderful last year of his life, Jimmy was able to show people what a difference Christ can make in one's life and in the lives of others. I would not be writing to you today were it not for the inspiration I received from hearing Jimmy's story of redemption.

In a sense, I feel even more blessed than Jimmy Duke. It has now been over a decade since I came back to Christianity. I've been blessed with a nationally syndicated column and with several book contracts. Those blessings have afforded me an opportunity to share the truth with those who are being led astray in a world captivated by lies and deceit.

But you are more fortunate than any of us. You have your whole life in front of you. You were led astray during your first couple of years of college. But since we have been talking over the course of the last year, I've seen great changes in your outlook on life. I've seen things that have led me to believe that you are not going to squander large portions of your adult life as Mickey, Jimmy, and I did. Collectively, we wasted nearly a hundred years striking out in anger over things we did not understand, and reaching for things that were not really of any worth.

When writing to you, I've often thought about your father. He has spent nearly all of his life working at a blue collar job. He wanted to give you the college education he never had. But, as I'm sure he knows, there are some things in life a college education cannot teach. Sadly, many of those who call themselves teachers are determined to keep you from discovering the things you need to live a life that is worth living. It is not for lack of intelligence. It is for lack of humility. It is my hope that you will return to the teachings of your father and trust that he has more concern for your well-being than the tenured radicals you have encountered in college.

What you learned in your father's house might not be as enticing as some of the ideas you encounter in college. Indeed, the truth can sometimes seem like a rigid set of punitive commandments, but in reality, it is nothing less than a gift from God. It is His way of telling you what you really desire, so that you can live a life that is worth living. When you arrive at that Truth, you will find peace with your earthly father. You will also please your Heavenly Father, and you will cherish every day you wake up with the blessing of sharing the Truth with future generations.

Those who acknowledge the Truth will join the only Hall of Fame that really matters. It is not a place where men live in a state of perpetual rebellion. It is a place where angels live in a state of perpetual joy. Their joy is not in knowing what the future holds. Their joy is in knowing the One who holds the future.

The Silent Scream

Dear Zach,

I can't tell you how happy I was to read your letter. I can't imagine any better news than your decision to commit yourself to Christ, and I really appreciate your sharing your father's reaction with me. I hope (and pray) that your relationship with your parents will continue to heal and strengthen as you mature in faith and wisdom.

I thank God every day for my parents. I also occasionally thank God for my parents' friends. One of those special friends is a woman named Lisa Chambers. I've written to you before about the Chambers family. They were the people who lived in the apartment complex across the street from us when we moved to Clear Lake City, Texas, in the late 1960s.

I am going to tell you a story about Lisa Chambers now, because it's an excellent example of the kind of Christian witness I want you to be able to give. After moving away from Texas in 1985, I returned to Clear Lake in order to attend the ten-year reunion of the Clear Lake High School class of 1983. When I went home, Steve and Lisa Chambers were visiting from Atlanta, Georgia, where they had moved in the late 1970s. I was so glad Steve and Lisa had remained friends with my mother and father. In fact, they are still dear friends to this day.

One morning during that 1993 visit, Lisa Chambers sat down with me at breakfast for about fifteen minutes. She asked whether I had voted for Bill Clinton in 1992. I told her I had. She asked whether it bothered me that he was our first unequivocally pro-choice president. I told her it did not. Then she asked whether I was pro-choice. I told her I was.

Mrs. Chambers responded to my honest answers in a calm and calculated way that I now recognize as brilliant. She told me that one of her sons had a friend who worked at a crisis pregnancy center. From there, she began to talk about the impact that technology had upon women who were considering abortion. Then, she told me about a man named Bernard Nathanson. It was the first time I would hear his name. But it would not be the last.

Mrs. Chambers did not tell me that Bernard Nathanson was once an abortion doctor who co-founded the National Abortion Rights Action League, or NARAL. Nor did she tell me that he had once aborted one of his own children. But she did tell me he was a Jewish convert to Christianity who was a courageous pro-life advocate. She also told me about a film he had made in 1984. That film was called *The Silent Scream.*

Although it is only twenty-eight minutes long, *The Silent Scream* caused quite a firestorm when it was released. In the film, there is an ultrasound of an abortion as it is actually taking place. It is simply chilling to watch. It does more than just prove conclusively that the thing that is being aborted is a tiny human being rather than a lifeless clump of cells. It also shows that the tiny human being feels the pain of the abortion as it is taking place. It actually shows a tiny mouth opening as the baby screams in agony while being dismembered.

Mrs. Chambers took no more than a few minutes of my time as she explained to me that *The Silent Scream* proved—through medical technology, no less—that a baby feels pain as it is being aborted. After she was finished, she simply urged me to take the time to watch the movie. That was it.

For the life of me, I could not get the image of that baby out of my mind after Mrs. Chambers described how it cried out for help during an abortion. Note that this was long before I even saw *The Silent Scream*. Mrs. Chambers had brilliantly planted that image in my mind so that I could not avoid the central question of whether the object of the abortion is, in fact, a living human being.

It should go without saying that I eventually saw *The Silent Scream*. I was so moved by it that I eventually organized two showings of the movie on my campus. I even set up panels to discuss it afterwards. I invited pro-abortion feminists. None accepted the invitation.

The point of my writing to you about Mrs. Chambers has little to do with the substantive issue of abortion. I know you already agree with me that abortion is murder.

The real point of my telling you this story is to remind you that you do not always have to get into an argument in order to win a convert to your way of thinking—even on an issue that means a lot to you. Mrs. Chambers did not start an argument with me. Had she done so, I would not have listened to her. My heart was not in the right place, and she knew it. Instead, she decided she would simply plant a stone in my shoe.

Please remember this lesson and use it to your advantage. When someone you want to influence is simply not listening, go and find yourself a stone. Slip it into their shoe so that every time they take a step they will be reminded of it. Let their growing discomfort with their own positions cause them to stop and re-evaluate their thinking. You don't have to beat them over the head. You just have to leverage their own weight—the weight of their inner conscience—against them.

In the case of my discussion with Mrs. Chambers, she just needed fifteen minutes to start a great awakening in my conscience. I began to fundamentally rethink the issue of abortion. But I also began to think about larger issues as well. If life begins before birth, then does it extend after death? If life begins before a woman is aware she is pregnant, then how can she ever have the moral authority to take it? What is the origin of moral authority in the first place?

These are all important questions. As you know, they can lead to answers that truly change lives.

Killing Till

Dear Zach,

What you wrote me about how your life has been changing in the past month is truly phenomenal. It seems that God has been doing momentous things in your life this summer. As you grow in your rediscovered Christian faith, you're going to be thinking about how you are called to fight in the battle for the truths you now recognize—and ultimately for the Truth.

In my last letter I told you the story of how Mrs. Chambers managed to eventually change my mind about abortion by employing a method that was gentle, subtle, and very effective. But in the right circumstances, it can also be very effective to use more aggressive techniques of persuasion—to bring up arguments that can be called harsh and evidence that is truly horrifying to see.

To illustrate this point, I want draw your attention to the Emmett Till case, which involved the tragic death of a young black teenager at the hands of two white supremacists in the Mississippi Delta in 1955. I have recently decided to add it to the list of trials covered in my popular "Trials of the Century" course, which you have already completed here at UNC-Wilmington.

My own interest in the Till case began back in 1989, when I was attending graduate school just ninety miles away from where Till was murdered. In the summer of 2010, my interest in the case was revived quite unexpectedly when my friend John Stonestreet, the voice of Breakpoint Radio and a colleague at Summit Ministries, hit me with a stunning revelation: his wife Sarah is the granddaughter of Robert Smith, who was the lead prosecutor in the Emmett Till case.

As a result of my friendship with the Stonestreets, I was able to obtain and read numerous documents relating to the trial that were fortunately still in the possession of one of Robert Smith's surviving children, Sarah's father Fred. Reading the original local newspaper accounts and personal correspondence of the lead prosecutor provided fresh new insights into the Till murder case.

When I teach about the Till trial, I will be careful to tell students that there is much factual ambiguity regarding the events leading to the death of young Emmett. But there are some things we know for certain. Some of the most horrible facts of the case are simply beyond dispute.

It was late in the summer of 1955, at a time when racism was endemic—and sometimes lethal—in Mississippi. Young Emmett, at just fourteen years of age, had traveled from his home in Chicago to visit relatives living in the Mississippi Delta. After Emmett told his cousins that he had dated white women, there was a dare, and he ended up going into Bryant Grocery Store to ask twenty-one-year-old Carolyn Bryant for a date. This is where the factual ambiguity sets in. One account says that all Till did to offend Bryant was put money in her hand rather than placing it on the counter. This would have been a violation of the taboo against any kind of physical contact between black males and white females. Other accounts say that Till "wolf-whistled," asked Bryant for a date, and grabbed her around the waist (which would have been simple assault).

Regardless of the actual events in that store, what happened a few days later was an utterly shocking and unjustifiable crime against a minor. Till was abducted from the home of his great-uncle Moses Wright in the wee hours of the morning. His captors were Carolyn Bryant's husband, Roy, and J. W. Milam.

After the abduction, Till was brutally pistol-whipped—beaten so badly that one of his eyes popped out of its socket. Later, he was fatally shot in the head. A large fan was then attached to his body via barbed wire so that his corpse would sink to the bottom of the Tallahatchie River, where it was finally dumped.

Bryant and Milam were acquitted in September of 1955, just a few weeks after Till's murder. The double jeopardy clause of the Mississippi Constitution, based on the Fifth Amendment of the U.S. Constitution, barred a retrial.

Given the national media attention the case had garnered, Milam and Bryant figured they could cash in by selling the story. So they described the murder of Emmett Till to a reporter for *Look* magazine in a now-infamous 1956 interview. They thought they had nothing to lose, but they were wrong.

Milam had this to say of Emmett Till's last words on earth: "I stood there in that shed and listened to that n——r throw poison at me." Milam also claimed that he asked Till, "You still as good as I am?" to which he replied "Yeah." Finally, they report Milam's claim that he asked Till, "You still 'had' white women?" to which Till responded "Yeah."

Zach, I consider it unlikely that any of that dialogue actually took place. The only honest person who was on the scene was murdered. The two murderers were proven liars. After all, they had entered verdicts of not guilty and later confessed to being guilty. So their accounts cannot simply be presumed to be accurate.

Milam also had a strong motive to lie. Bryant and Milam knew they had been given a pass in the court of law. They thought they would be given a pass in the court of public opinion, too—especially if they appealed to white people's hatred and fear of "uppity" black people. But the murderers would not, in fact, be given a pass in the court of public opinion. Many whites in the Mississippi Delta were bothered by the brutality of the murder—and by the fact that it was perpetrated against a minor. Emmett Till's mother, in an act of unmitigated heroism, had demanded an open-casket funeral so the world was able to see young Emmett's one-eyed head, swollen to over twice its normal size. It looked like a part of a grotesque costume made for a Hollywood horror film. But it was not. It was real. And it evoked justifiable outrage.

I do not believe I am alone in suspecting that the Milam account of Till's last words was an outright fabrication. Milam wanted it to look as if Emmett had brought the murder on himself by boasting, and that perhaps a little humility could have saved him. Milam was trying to exonerate himself in white Southerners' opinions by painting himself as an agent of the intimidation that forced black people themselves to accept white supremacy, and, perhaps more importantly, by portraying himself as a valiant defender of the taboo against interracial relationships between black men and white women.

But Milam failed on both counts. In fact, his efforts backfired.

Milam and Bryant were unable to get loans to do business in the Mississippi Delta after giving that interview. Both of them had to leave the area in shame. And both Milam and Bryant saw their marriages end in the wake of the trial. Their wives decided to leave them and start lives free of the stigma of being married to murderous white supremacists. The South was beginning to change, although very slowly.

Racist violence declined in popularity in the wake of the Till open-casket funeral, which had forced the whole nation to confront the horror of lynching. The name of one woman who was moved by that open casket should be familiar to you. I am referring to Rosa Parks. After she saw Emmet Till's horribly disfigured face, she was inspired to refuse to give up her seat to a white person on a public bus in Montgomery, Alabama. In death, Emmett had helped launch the Civil Rights Movement.

In many respects, things have gotten better since Emmet Till's death. And they will get better still. (Not that you'd know that from listening to progressives. They always seek to enhance the allure of their future utopia by exaggerating the misery of our present reality. They're also not big fans of the United States Constitution, which they frequently point out was written and ratified by a bunch of racist slave owners. But the First Amendment played a major role in the success of the Civil Rights Movement. Without a free press, the corpse of Emmet Till would have moved few people.)

The legacy of Emmett Till continues to resonate in the battle against another human rights abuse. The Center for Bioethical Reform has started the Genocide Awareness Project (GAP), using the same logic behind the decision to open Emmett Till's casket. In fact, they specifically cite Till's open-casket funeral and its after-effects as a justification for GAP.

The GAP mission involves going to college campuses and putting up pictures of aborted children behind tables where students can get information about abortion. GAP volunteers talk to students about the racist origins of Planned Parenthood and the disproportionate effect abortion has had on the black community. As a result, there is a new civil rights movement forming in America. It focuses on the senseless murder of children much younger and even more helpless than Emmett Till.

Men without Spines

Zach,

What you wrote me about how your life has been changing in the past month is truly phenomenal. It seems that God has been doing momentous things this summer. Congratulations on being ready to start your senior year in college with a new sense of your mission to defend the Truth in a hostile environment. Today I'm going to write you on that subject.

It is difficult for me to imagine many of today's young men as grandfathers. It is especially difficult when I think of the last time I saw my grandfather alive. It was one afternoon during the summer of '77 when we were in Birmingham, Alabama. We had all planned to go to the mall to shop for the entire afternoon. But that was before my grandfather fell and hit an iron furnace, badly cutting the back of his left hand. I can still see him standing in the doorway waving goodbye as we left without him. His right hand was clutching the walker he had used for almost as long as I knew him.

My grandfather used that walker because there was a piece of shrapnel lodged somewhere in his lower back. It was there because a hand grenade had gone off near him when he was fighting in France during World War I. He was only nineteen years old when it happened.

He used to tell us war stories—including the time he lied about his age in order to join the U.S. Army fighting against Pancho Villa somewhere down in Texas. That was some time around 1916. He was actually old enough to fight legally in the First World War. He spent his nineteenth birthday in a foxhole in France getting trench foot. It was shortly thereafter that he came out of that same foxhole and got a piece of a hand grenade lodged in his back.

The difference between men in my grandfather's generation and young men today can be roughly summarized as follows: **Men in my grandfather's generation were willing to lie to get into a fight, even if it meant they might lose their lives. Men in today's generation are**

willing to lie to avoid a fight, even when their lives are not remotely in jeopardy.

I see this contrast every summer when I come out to Colorado to teach at Summit Ministries. The young women are always fired up and ready to advance the truth in our often contentious cultural wars. But many of the young men will latch on to any Bible verse and twist its meaning until they can justify doing absolutely nothing. That assumes, of course, that you consider playing video games to be doing nothing. The only battles in which some of these males engage are fought by pointing a joystick at a television screen. (I know they don't call them "joysticks" any more but I think you understand my point.)

When young Christian males challenge my sometimes aggressive tactics in the campus cultural wars, they tend to rely on the same handful of Bible verses:

1. **Matthew 5:39.** In this oft-quoted verse, Jesus tells us to turn and offer the other cheek after someone strikes us.

2. **Luke 6:29 and Matthew 5:40.** In these parallel verses, Jesus tells us to give someone our cloak when he asks for it. In fact, Jesus tells us we should also give the person our tunic—literally, the shirt off our back—and if someone sues us for our shirt, we should hand over our coat as well.

3. **Romans 12:18.** In this verse, Paul tells us that we should, whenever possible, live in peace with all people.

These verses are often specifically brought up by young Christian men who object to Christian involvement in litigation. I respond to the first objection by suggesting that turning the other cheek is the appropriate Christian response to personal insults. I concur fully with young men who say we should not respond to personal insults.

But it certainly does not follow that Christians should never take a stand for Jesus. If we never stand up for Jesus, no one is ever likely to slap our faces or insult us in any way. Clearly, those who use this verse to justify total passivity are stretching the verse beyond all recognition.

I respond to the second objection—the shirt-off-our-back objection—by asking this fundamental question: We have a right to give away our own tunic, but does that mean we also have a right to give away somebody else's?

The question is a fair one in this context because the point of litigation is so often to assert the rights of college Christian groups. For example, a few years ago the Student Government Association at Georgia Tech told a Christian group's leaders that they could not be funded from student activity fees—which members of the group had paid along with all other students—because they are a religious group and only secular groups could receive funding. Therefore,

Christians were paying to support all of the secular groups but not getting any money themselves. The problem was that the United States Supreme Court had ruled (six years earlier!) that this was illegal.

When approached about asserting the constitutional rights of the Christian group, the group's leader refused to even consider litigation. So, in effect, he gave away the rights of every other person in the group. In fact, it's worse than that. He gave away the rights of every member of every *other* Christian group on campus, too. Did Jesus really want him to give away the rights of other people—basic constitutional rights to freedom of speech and religion that were earned by other people fighting wars in service to our country? I certainly don't think so, and I doubt my grandfather would think so either.

Before you give your answer, consider this: If all secular groups are funded and no Christian groups are funded, then doesn't that mean that only the secular worldview is advanced with student fees? Doesn't that mean that souls will be lost because of Christian apathy? Is it really possible to square this with the Great Commission?

I respond to the final objection—from Romans 12:18—by reminding people that Paul told us we should live in peace with others *whenever possible*. But sometimes that just isn't possible. Prior to every lawsuit I am ever involved in, a letter is sent to the offending party explaining the exact nature of the perceived legal transgression. This is done in private so that the offending party is spared the prospect of humiliation. They have an opportunity to back out before being embarrassed in any way—either in the court of public opinion or in a court of law.

But the heart of the offending party is often hardened by the mere suggestion that they may be doing wrong. In fact, sometimes they respond with hostility, daring Christian lawyers to proceed with litigation—and so they do.

A large part of the problem comes from the law of qualified immunity. Under qualified immunity, government officials who are put in charge of enforcing government regulations are given protection from paying personal damages in the event of litigation. This would seem to make intuitive sense. If it became too easy to sue government officials and make them personally pay damages, no one would want to take on the role of public servant. But qualified immunity is only supposed to apply when a government official is acting in "reasonable reliance" on the law. In other words, if the official violated the law but was a) in fact unaware of it and also b) *reasonably* unaware of it, then the official cannot be sued.

The key to assessing reasonableness is determining whether the average, ordinary person would have been aware of the legal violation. If the average person would not have been aware that they were violating the law, then why punish the officials who violated it? Society has no interest in deterring reasonable conduct—only unreasonable conduct. The problem, of course, is that people will often try to "play dumb" and pretend they were unaware of wrong-doing. Enter Jonathan Lopez.

I first heard of Jonathan Lopez when he was a nineteen-year-old student at Los Angeles Community College (LACC). Some time during the fall semester of 2009, he was asked to give an informative speech on a topic of his own choosing. He chose to give his speech on the impact God has had on his life. That's when the trouble began.

Jonathan's professor, John Matteson, was fine with the speech until Lopez read a Bible verse dealing with marriage—specifically, affirming the traditional definition of marriage. When Jonathan read that verse, Professor Matteson jumped up out of his chair and called Lopez a "fascist bastard." When the startled students turned toward Matteson, he simply asked them whether anyone had been offended by what Jonathan had said. When no one reported being offended, Matteson became very angry and dismissed the entire class.

The walk from the podium back to his seat in the rear of the class must have been a long one for Jonathan Lopez. But he had to make it because he needed to gather his belongings before heading to his next class. When he leaned down to pick up his book bag he noticed that it was unzipped. Professor Matteson had slipped a piece of paper into the bag. On that piece of paper was only one sentence: "Ask God what your grade is."

Jonathan did the right thing in response to Professor Matteson's mocking refusal to grade his speech. He went to see an LACC administrator about resolving the issue so he could get credit for the speech and, hopefully, pass the class. But his meeting with the administrator was not successful. The speech remained ungraded, and the situation remained unresolved.

That is when Jonathan decided to call my good friends at the Alliance Defense Fund (ADF). They immediately took the case and wrote a letter to the president of LACC. It was a clear, concise letter explaining that Jonathan Lopez had been punished for simply exercising his rights to the free exercise of religion under the United States Constitution. Remember that Matteson never told Lopez he could not quote a verse from the Bible. He was being punished for allegedly offending students, which is a violation of the LACC speech code.

The ADF could have simply filed suit. But they wrote the letter first—thus remaining in compliance with the Apostle Paul's instruction that we are supposed to live at peace with everyone whenever possible. But in this case, peace was not possible. The president of LACC reacted arrogantly by simply giving the ADF the phone number of the Office of the Attorney General of California. At the time of the incident, the California Attorney General was none other than Jerry Brown—a vocal supporter of same-sex marriage.

In other words, LACC simply flipped the ADF the middle finger. So ADF sued on behalf of Jonathan Lopez. His efforts paid off. A federal court granted an injunction and struck down the LACC speech code in a matter of weeks. But the case was far from over.

The LACC administration dug in its heels and appealed the decision to the Ninth Circuit Court of Appeals—the most liberal circuit in the United States. Zach, you will recall that this is the circuit which, among other things, has ruled against the use of the phrase "under God" in the Pledge of Allegiance.

It is unsurprising that the Ninth Circuit decided to overrule Jonathan's free speech victory. If there is one surprising aspect of the appeal, it is that the judges were not angry with John Matteson for using the word "God" in his infamous "Ask God what your grade is" note to Mr. Lopez. After all, the Ninth Circuit wants to ban all other references to God in the classroom. I guess some uses of the word "God" are more equal than others.

Jonathan and the ADF appealed the case to the United States Supreme Court, which unfortunately refused to grant certiorari. But the ADF and other brave Christian plaintiffs continue to defend freedom of speech on campus by means of our legal system—and they are right to do so.

Remember that Jonathan tried everything in his power to resolve this conflict peacefully—in accordance with Romans 12:18. He went and spoke to the administration. He had lawyers write a well-reasoned letter. He only sued because he was, in effect, asked to do so by a college administration that rudely thumbed its nose at him. After he won a quick legal victory, it was the anti-Christian defenders of the speech code who revived the lawsuit on appeal.

You have to respect Jonathan Lopez for showing tremendous courage since the beginning of this saga when he was just a nineteen-year old student simply trying to give a speech of encouragement and hope (not Hope). Since then, he has been mocked, insulted, and ridiculed by people who have far greater authority and influence than he does. But I suspect that, in the final analysis, all of their names will be forgotten, and he will be remembered as an exceptional man in an unexceptional generation.

We can seldom control the manner in which we will be remembered. But we all must decide whether we will live lives that will be worth remembering. I'll never forget my grandfather because he began taking on the forces of evil and living as a warrior when he was only a teenager. For the same reason, I'll never forget the name of Jonathan Lopez. I hope you'll remember him, just as I hope that one day you'll be remembered for standing tall among a generation that is shrinking.

How to Answer a False Accusation of Homophobia

Zach,

In case you haven't already noticed, the tolerance of the "tolerant" generally doesn't run very deep. Any intellectual opposition drives leftists to extremely hostile behavior. If you criticize them or even express disagreement with their beliefs, you can expect to encounter scorn, derision, and name-calling. So you need to be ready to deal with their attacks. Let's take the common accusation of "homophobia" as an example.

The term "homophobia" is nothing if not judgmental. It is used in an attempt to portray opponents of the gay rights movement as somehow morally deficient. But it goes beyond that to imply that the opponent of gay rights is somehow mentally disturbed. That is quite an interesting development, when one considers the history of conflict between the gay rights movement and the leadership of the American Psychiatric Association (APA).

Although it may be difficult for you to imagine, the APA characterized homosexuality as a mental illness as recently as the early 1970s. But an organized political coalition within the APA managed to have homosexuality declassified as a mental illness. They got homosexuality removed from the comprehensive list of mental illnesses known as the Diagnostic and Statistical Manual, or DSM, and eventually they set about making opposition to homosexuality look like a mental illness.

Approximately twenty years after homosexuality was declassified from the DSM, the word "homophobia" began to creep into the national debate over gay rights issues. The term first came to the attention of many Americans in 1993 soon after Bill Clinton took office as our forty-second president, in the context of the debate over Clinton's "Don't ask, don't tell" policy allowing gays to serve in the military, although not openly.

It is conceivable that a person could oppose gays in the military out of some irrational fear of homosexuals. That is what the term "homophobia" originally meant—not just a fear of homosexuals but an irrational one. But that is no

longer what the term means. It now no longer describes a
fear at all, but rather any sort of opposition to the gay rights
agenda. Let me give you an example.

I recently wrote a column criticizing my university for
releasing a list of "gay-friendly" churches in the Wilmington area. I was disappointed with the list for several reasons.
One reason was that a government institution—the UNC-
Wilmington LGBTQIA Office—was helping private citizens
select churches, and that they were doing so using taxpayer
resources. It also bothered me that they only selected five
churches as "gay-friendly." The implication was that the
other 245 Wilmington churches were somehow "unfriendly"
towards gay people. I don't think that's true. The response
to my column was predictable: I was accused of being a
"homophobe."

I asked my accusers these two questions (using a form
email response):

1. What exactly does homophobia mean?
2. What does homophobia have to do with the
    situation at hand?

Unsurprisingly, I did not receive a single response to either
of my very simple questions. The reason for that is also
very simple: homophobia is a loosely defined term that is
used to describe any opposition to the gay political agenda.
It is broadly and carelessly used against those who are

not afraid of speaking out against the gay agenda in the hopes that they will be silenced because they are afraid to speak out. In other words, the people who complain about "homophobia" are not really fighting against fear of gay people. They are deliberately encouraging it.

Matthew 23

Dear Zach,

I was once challenged by a couple of young Christian men who were dissatisfied with my response to a controversy involving the promotion of the transgender movement at my university. The controversy began when the feminist leadership of my department (The UNC-Wilmington Sociology and Criminology Department) sponsored a film that encourages young people who are considering having sex changes. I responded with a scathingly sarcastic editorial ridiculing them for doing so. I'll explain why I did that after I explain why the feminists did what they did.

The motivation for encouraging sex change operations is rooted in a feminist agenda that denies any significant biological differences between the sexes. The feminists want to show that any unequal outcomes between men and women are due to patriarchal oppression. Therefore, they try to show that all differences between the sexes are merely "socially constructed." This is done in order to garner political support for massive social engineering. In the end, it produces a society with two kinds of people: women and women with penises.

Zach, I want to be clear on two preliminary matters:

1. I support the right of feminists to argue completely ridiculous positions. If the feminists are too dense to recognize the many and profound biological differences between the sexes, so be it. The more often they make absurd arguments, the easier it is for me to destroy the credibility of those who murder innocent children in the name of "choice." In other words, I will defend vigorously their right to make fools of themselves.

2. When these feminists engage in speech that is both a) knowingly false, and b) harmful to other people, I will use a lethal combination of truth and ridicule to destroy their credibility. I do not do this out of a desire to hurt the feminists. I do

it out of a desire to help the people the feminists
are hurting.

Although the use of ridicule can be effective, many
Christians shy away from using it under any circumstances.
They do this largely because of a misunderstanding of what
the Apostle Paul said in the Epistle to the Ephesians. In
Ephesians 4:15, Paul issued a command to speak the truth
in love. But those who know anything about the manner in
which the Bible was written know that it was not divided
into verses originally—in fact, not until hundreds of years
after it had been written. If we read individual verses of
the Bible while ignoring surrounding verses in the larger
paragraph—or chapter or book—we are likely to fall prey to
mistakes of interpretation.

To put things in context, Ephesians 4:15 is part of a
larger section of Paul's Epistle to the Ephesians that exhorts
Christians to speak kindly to one another in the process of
resolving church conflict. But many Christians misinterpret
the passage in two important ways: 1) by assuming that the
passage applies to all Christian communication in all con-
texts, and 2) by thinking that it precludes any and all use of
ridicule.

Such an interpretation is demonstrably false unless we
want to believe that one part of the Bible contradicts another
part of the Bible. Since Jesus himself uses ridicule—most
notably in Matthew 23—it would be a contradiction to assert

the existence of a Biblical ban on ridicule. Nonetheless, Jesus did not use ridicule toward everyone. In fact, Jesus seems to have reserved it exclusively for a special group of teachers called the Pharisees, who incurred his wrath more often than anyone else featured in the Gospel accounts.

Jesus' wrath was directed especially towards the Pharisees' hypocrisy—an often-used but seldom understood term. For Jesus, the term hypocrisy seems to mean more than simply failing to live up to the standards one articulates. Although that is a common understanding of the term, it really is meaningless. Everyone fails to live up to his own standards—at least occasionally. Therefore, under this definition, anyone can be deemed a hypocrite. If the term includes everyone, it excludes no one and is therefore meaningless.

The Pharisees were different in that they did not even believe the things they were saying. That is the true definition of a hypocrite: **One who preaches something that he does not practice *and* that he does not even believe.** It is a dangerous trait for a teacher to possess. Put simply, it is bad when people speak untruths, but it is worse when they do so knowingly—and it is simply inexcusable when they call themselves "teachers."

So Jesus would certainly have us speak the truth in love to fellow Christians when we have disagreements. That is what I am trying to do now with young Christians who believe we should always abstain from litigation and also abstain from the use of ridicule. Thankfully, it is easy for us to tell the difference between a Christian brother or sister and a hardened Pharisee.

The people in my department who have no qualms about encouraging minors to get sex changes can rightly be called Pharisees. They want us to believe that there are two kinds of people in the world—as I said before, women and women with penises (and if you would like to be the former rather than the latter, the solution is just a few quick trips to the doctor, or so they say).

These Pharisees whom I have ridiculed do not misrepresent the truth innocently. They knowingly lie about biological differences between the sexes. As I stated earlier in my letter, they do so in order to attribute any differences in outcome between the sexes to "patriarchal oppression." This, in turn, is done to facilitate more social engineering, which creates more jobs for self-proclaimed social engineers. Of course, they are the social engineers who would benefit from those jobs.

Lying to students about basic biological facts in order to encourage genital mutilation is bad. The only thing worse would be lying about basic biological facts in order to encourage murder. As you will recall from our previous correspondence on abortion, the modern-day Pharisees are not above that either.

How Great
Mao Art

Zach,

Once again, I'm packing in preparation to return to Colorado for the summer. Congratulations on your impending graduation. I've enjoyed discussing these issues with you in greater depth in my office hours this year, as well as in our correspondence. Now you're ready to take off into "the real world," where you'll find plenty of opportunities to use the debating skills—and the courage—that you've honed here on campus. I want to send you just one final letter, about the deep contrast between the progressive worldview you have left behind and the Christian world-view you have chosen to accept.

A student in California once wrote to tap into my thoughts about Marxism and how it relates to Christianity. Specifically, he asked whether Jesus, if he returned today, would be a capitalist or a socialist. I recommended that the student read *Money, Greed, and God* by Jay Richards. His is the best book I've read on this issue, which should not be a very difficult one for most Christians to resolve.

There is some confusion on this topic as a result of some misinterpreted passages in the Book of Acts. Those passages describe an early congregation of Christians that voluntarily shared all things and all possessions as common property. See Acts 4:32–37 for a full overview and proper context.

Unfortunately, some Christians equate the voluntary sharing of property initiated by individuals with the involuntary sharing of property compelled by governments. In fact, the distinction is no less subtle than the distinction between charity and theft.

It is also worth noting, before we proceed, that the assumption of private ownership of property is implicit in the Tenth Commandment, which tells us not to covet other people's property. Coveting is not possible if all property is shared and there is no private ownership.

Put simply, forcing people to turn over their property at the point of a gun destroys Christian charity. There can be no charity without free will. Furthermore, if one were to insist on calling forcibly redistributed wealth "charity," there is still an additional problem—socialism reduces wealth and, hence, reduces the absolute volume of one's giving.

Capitalism is the only known economic system that actually produces wealth. Therefore, it increases the size of one's tithe—as well as making it possible to give freely in the first place.

But there is an even better reason for Christians not to abandon capitalism for Marxism. Look at the following list of twentieth-century regimes that committed at least a million murders in the name of utopian Marxism:

China	65 million
U.S.S.R.	20 million
North Korea	2 million
Cambodia	2 million
Afghanistan	1.5 million
Vietnam	1 million

Before we condemn capitalism as falling short of creating heaven on earth, we must admit that Marxism has come close to creating hell on earth. But heaven is not an option here on earth. We must simply choose the best available alternative—and as you can see from the statistics above, Marxism is not a good alternative.

Nonetheless, our country has moved in the direction of socialism over the last few decades, and the consequences of our socialist War on Poverty have been devastating. In 1965, the illegitimacy rate was 24 percent among blacks and 3 percent among whites. Within twenty-five years it had risen to 64 percent among blacks and 18 percent among whites.

Surely Jesus would not approve of the socialist policies that have so crippled the American family in recent decades. It seems that those policies have had the effect of weakening the basic family structure that is established in the Bible.

But why are the results of socialism always so bad? I think it is fair to say that socialism is largely a rebellion against the Judeo-Christian view of human nature that is established very clearly in the Bible—specifically, in the third chapter of Genesis.

One cannot resolve the discrepancy between the view that man is fallen and in need of the redemptive power of Christ with the view that man is perfectible and in need of the redemptive power of government.

As I have said before, the fundamental mischaracterization of human nature has consequences. One of those consequences is policies that de-incentivize work. The assertion that work has significant intrinsic value to God is quite obvious and has a sound Biblical basis. God had Adam and Eve working in the Garden of Eden even before sin was introduced into the world.

After Christ returns, we are told that people will beat their swords into plowshares and spears into pruning hooks. In other words, people will be expected to work and to be productive. Godly economic policies are ones that encourage productivity, not sloth.

Our War on Poverty is not one that lives up to that standard. It has been more like a War on Productivity. It is no wonder that grown men who will not work to support themselves are also abandoning their children in record numbers.

In *The Wealth of Nations*, Adam Smith said that capitalism would work best among people possessed of moral resources. Such moral restraints would keep their self-interest from becoming unfettered greed. This is consistent with what the Apostle Paul said in Philippians 2:4 when he called on us to balance our self-interest with the interests of others.

We will never be able, as mere mortals, to bring about heaven on earth. But we can prevent hell on earth by basing our economy on Christian capitalism, not Marxist atheism. Even Friedrich Nietzsche understood that if God is dead, then chaos ensues—and in the end, the only redistribution of wealth comes at the hands of thieves, burglars, and brigands.

The basic choice that we face in every area of life is the same—whether we're talking about politics, family life, economics, gender roles, racism, crime, or poverty. Man is either an accident of nature whose choices are determined

236 LETTERS TO A YOUNG PROGRESSIVE

by his circumstances—so that we only need to tear society apart and remake it, in order to cure every problem and create a perfect world—or else a fallen creature who has used free will to rebel against a loving Creator and his moral law, which is written on human hearts so that we'll never be happy (or even reliably in touch with reality) unless we acknowledge his law and return to his love.

Zach, this is the intellectual and spiritual battle we're in. The good thing is, you've already picked the right side.

Acknowledgments

Special thanks to my old high school principal Henry Thornton. I remember when he got ahold of me in high school and took an interest in the fact that I was wasting my life by not engaging my mind or honing my reading and writing skills. I appreciate the fact that he sparked my interest in reading and writing at a time when I could not care less about school. When I finally turned things around—a couple of years after graduating near the bottom of my high school class—he was there to cheer me on every step of the way. When it finally appeared that I would graduate from college, there was no masking his enthusiasm.

It was contagious, and it inspired me. I am so glad we have reconnected over the last few months. It has really put this project into perspective.

I owe special thanks to David A. Noebel, the founder of Summit Ministries, who got me out to Colorado for the first time back in 2008. By 2010, I was spending entire summers speaking at Summit Ministries. That gave me the time to get away and write this book. It also gave me the exact perspective I would need to write it. In 1962, "Doc" Noebel started Summit Ministries as a two-week Christian worldview camp. The idea behind the camp is that students can come out for a couple of weeks to study theology, philosophy, and current events. They do not merely examine issues within the framework of a Christian worldview. They also examine them in relation to other worldviews. Many students come out here as young as age sixteen, and because of the camp they are less likely to fall away from their faith once they go to college. In other words, because of Doc's ministry there are fewer young people wasting their lives being angry over things that aren't really true. The ministry has been a great inspiration to me.

I also want to thank Gabe Schneider and Suzanne Nichols Kroleski for their editorial assistance. The staffers at Summit Ministries are the greatest. I thank them for taking time out from their duties to assist me with mine. They helped get the manuscript ready to submit to Regnery.

Speaking of Regnery, signing with them was the second best decision I ever made as a writer. Editors Harry Crocker and Elizabeth Kantor vastly improved the manuscript in the months leading to publication. I think that in its final form it will be far more likely to move readers to consider what is at stake in the current culture war. That is important to me. I did not write this book to entertain people. I wrote it for a lost generation and the parents who need help reaching them. Lives are at stake here. Elizabeth gets that. So does Harry.

The best decision I ever made as a writer was choosing D. J. Snell as an agent. Like many of my best decisions, it was done at the suggestion of my good friend and wise counselor David French. D.J. and David are pretty bright for a couple Harvard Law graduates. I'm glad I retained them both.

Index

Los Angeles Community
    College, 217–19
Ludacris, 34–35
Lynch, Michael, 38, 40–41

M

MacCallum, Martha, 150
Manson, Charles, 1, 6, 9,
    11–12, 77
Mantle, Mickey, 191–95
marriage,
    polygamy and, 82–83
    same-sex (gay), 79, 81–84,
        218
    traditional, 79, 81–84, 217
Marxism, 15. *See also* com-
    munism; socialism,
    atheism and, 235
    cultural, 35
    discredited by history
        and logic, 17
    economics and, 6–7, 8, 12
    lower standard of living
        and, 11
    murders in name of, 233
Marx, Karl, 6, 14–15
Matteson, John, 217–19
Media Matters, 3

Mensa International, 166
*Merriam-Webster Diction-
    ary,* 159
Milam, J. W., 205–8
Miller, Tiffany, 132–33, 136
Mississippi Constitution,
    206
Mississippi State Univer-
    sity (MSU), 29–31, 131,
    184
"mistake of fact," 80
"mistake of law," 80–81
Modest Proposal (Swift), 51
Money, Greed, and God
    (Richards), 232
moral equivalence, 11–12
moral law, 180–81
moral relativism, 11–12, 179–
    80
    discredited by history
        and logic, 17
Mormons, 82–83
Moseley, Winston, 98
Murdoch, Rupert, 170

N

NAACP, 158
NASA, 183

as defense of abortion,
    51–52
Jonathan Swift's solu-
    tion for, 51
LBJ on, 100
seen by progressives as
    major cause of crime
    by, 97, 107
War on, 100, 234–35
prison, 9, 178–81
progressives, progressivism,
    affirmative action's
        lower performance
        supported by, 27
    atheism and, 172
    criminal justice system
        study errors and,
        37–43
    fascists and, 160, 217
    gun control and, 109–10,
        132–33
    personhood of defense-
        less unborn denied by,
        56
    poverty seen as major
        cause of crime by, 97,
        107
    racism and, 17–22, 37–43

rape victims used for
    political purposes by,
    56
theories of crime and
    delinquency of, 85–90,
    92–95, 107
truth about, 16
U.S. Constitution and,
    208–9
"proletariat," 15
*Pro-life Answers to Pro-
    choice Arguments*
    (Alcorn), 65
Protestant Reformation,
    153
Purdy, Larry, 24

Q

qualified immunity, 216
quid pro quo harassment,
    31

R

Race and Criminal Justice
    (Lynch and Patterson),
    38, 40–42
racism, 17–22
    changed definition of, 18